— Running Your Own —
WORD PROCESSING SERVICE

Running Your Own

WORD PROCESSING SERVICE

Second Edition

Doreen Huntley

KOGAN PAGE

To Peter

First published in 1987 entitled *Running Your Own Typing Service*
Second edition 1991

Apart from any fair dealing for the purposes of research or private study, or criticism or review, as permitted under the Copyright, Designs and Patents Act, 1988, this publication may only be reproduced, stored or transmitted, in any form or by any means, with the prior permission in writing of the publishers, or in the case of reprographic reproduction in accordance with the terms of licences issued by the Copyright Licensing Agency. Enquiries concerning reproduction outside those terms should be sent to the publishers at the undermentioned address:

Kogan Page Limited
120 Pentonville Road
London N1 9JN

© Doreen Huntley 1987, 1991

British Library Cataloguing in Publication Data

A CIP record for this book is available from the British Library.

ISBN 0-7494-0344-6

Typeset by DP Photosetting, Aylesbury, Bucks
Printed and bound in Great Britain by
Biddles Ltd, Guildford

Contents

Preface to the Second Edition   **9**

Introduction   **11**
    Who can run a word-processing service? 11;
Who needs a word-processing service? 12;
What will it involve? 13; How far do you
need to commit yourself? 13; Your chances
of success 14

1. Look Before You Leap   **17**
    Are you the type? 17; Skills and abilities 21;
Running a business from home 24;
Essential start-up equipment 25; Start-up
costs 26

2. Planning Your Strategy   **28**
    Assessing the demand in your area 28;
What kind of service will you operate? 31;
How much time have you got? 33; Your
financial plan 34; Going it alone or in
partnership? 37

3. Starting Your Business   **40**
    Legal requirements – people you need to
inform 40; Your home 40; Choosing and
using a business name 43; Bookkeeping 44;
Insurance 45; Help and advice for new
businesses 46

4. Money Matters: Finance and Accounting   **48**
    Raising money 48; A business bank account
50; Keeping records 51; Annual accounts
54; Income tax 58; National Insurance 59;
What to send the tax inspector 61; Value
added tax 62; Changes in income tax,
National Insurance and VAT 64; Pensions
64; Pricing, costing and estimating 65

5. Sell Yourself! Marketing Your Service — 69
Advertising 69; Direct mail 73; Word of mouth recommendation 74; Business cards 75; Special offers 76; Marketing is more than simply selling your service 76; Your personal image 77

6. Tools of the Trade — 79
Setting up your office 79; Selecting and purchasing 'capital' equipment 80; Hiring or leasing equipment 110; Renewable supplies 111; Checklist of start-up supplies 112

7. Daily Operation of the Business — 114
Organising your time 114; Dealing with customers 119; Alterations, corrections and mistakes 125; Flexibility – go with your customers 127; Daily money matters 129; A checklist to help your word-processing service run smoothly 133

8. New Horizons: Expanding into New Fields — 135
Photocopying 135; Collection and delivery 135; 'Mobile' secretary 136; Bookkeeping 137; Telephone answering 138; Computerised business services 139; Electronic communications services 140; Facsimile 140; Audio-typing 141; Desktop publishing 142; Other services 145

9. How to Cope with Your Growing Business — 148
Subcontracting 148; Going into partnership 152

10. Starting an Office Services Bureau — 155
Bringing in the professionals 155; Buying an existing bureau 158; Starting afresh 159; Costing, pricing and estimating 163

11. Taking on Staff — 164
Selecting staff 164; Contracts of employment 166; Pay, tax and National Insurance 167; Hours of work, holidays and leave of absence 167; Good working relations 168; Employment legislation 169; Health and safety 169

12. Useful Addresses	**170**
13. Further Reading	**173**
Appendix	**179**
Guide to Layout and Sample Formats	
Index	**189**

Preface to the Second Edition

How times have changed! The first edition of this book was entitled *Running Your Own Typing Service* and only brief mention was made of developing a business based on word-processing rather than typewriting skills. Such has been the boom in word-processing, computing and information technology in the past few years that an extensive revision of the original text was called for. Although typewriters are far from obsolete (most businesses still use them – often in addition to word processors) the advantages of word-processing are so great, and the relative costs of purchasing the necessary equipment now so low, that anyone setting up a small office services business should seriously consider buying a word-processing package rather than a typewriter.

If you have already been trained to use a word processor, this may seem like sensible advice. However, if your keyboard skills were acquired by learning to type on a manual, electric or electronic typewriter, don't despair. Word-processing is easier than it sounds (or looks) and can be self-taught with little difficulty.

As well as providing advice on setting up and running a word-processing service, the new edition has been completely revised and updated to take account of changes in legislation, taxation, National Insurance, VAT registration and so on.

Doreen Huntley
Preston, 1991

Introduction

Running a word-processing (WP) or typing service must be one of the easiest ways to make money at home. The business can be as small, or as large, as you like; it can be fitted around the needs of housework/children, full- or part-time employment and other commitments and, once established, can provide a useful regular income for a relatively modest outlay.

This practical guide sets out to show how keyboard skills can be cheaply and easily put to use in the setting up and running of a small home-based business. Later chapters show how to cope as your business grows, how to expand and develop your service and, ultimately, how to set up your own office services agency. You have already taken the first essential step by seeking advice and information. So many small businesses fail simply through lack of preliminary planning. The time spent thinking about the service you wish to offer, how best to market it and what your commitment is going to be, can make all the difference between success and failure.

Who can run a word-processing service?

Nowadays, many skilled typists and WP operators find themselves out of work for one reason or another – the advent of children, disability, retirement, redundancy and so on. Although the vast majority of these are likely to be women, a growing proportion of men are trained in keyboard skills and office practice and there is no reason why they should not be just as successful in running their own word-processing service as their more traditional female counterparts. Provided you have the necessary skills, have (or can acquire) the basic equipment and can organise yourself effectively, you can run a word-processing service.

Many people are now trained to use a word processor; however, skilled typists who have no experience of WP technology should be able to cope equally well. The transition from typewriter to word processor is really not as great as many people imagine. Besides, even trained WP operators will almost certainly have to learn to use a different WP system in their own business, so some element of self-training or retraining is likely to be essential.

You don't need to dedicate all your time to operating a small home-based word-processing service. One full-time college librarian, who already had a home computer, printer and word-processing program for her personal use, decided to take in overflow work from a local business services agency (as well as the occasional dissertation from the students at her college). In this way, she acquired a small, fairly regular, part-time income for very little outlay. In one sense, you could say she was 'testing the water', and her abilities as a business woman, without losing the security of a full-time job. When she retired a few years later, she upgraded her equipment and established a part-time word-processing service of her own which supplemented her pension and occupied her spare time.

At the other extreme are two young women who, after acquiring all the necessary secretarial skills at college, found that they could not get the kind of jobs they wanted. They formed a partnership, bought a word processor (one of them already owned a typewriter) and started a business in a bedroom of their flat. After several months of hard work and determined marketing, their word-processing business took off. Eighteen months later they decided to open a secretarial agency and they haven't looked back since.

Between these two extremes are the many people who are somewhat restricted in the number of hours they have available for work – the housewife with children at school, the new mother, the part-time worker with hours to spare, the student wishing to work during the long summer holidays and so on. Whoever you are and whatever your circumstances, you can, with a little luck, plenty of common sense and lots of enthusiastic determination, run a successful home-based word-processing service.

Who needs a word-processing service?

Typing and word-processing are skills which are always needed by someone somewhere. Polytechnic, college and university students are required to submit typewritten theses and dissertations, so if you live near one of these institutions, your services are likely to be in great demand. Many small businesses cannot afford their own clerical staff and will often be delighted to have someone to prepare invoices, accounts, letters and so on. If you live in a rural area, you may find that business people and farmers will be pleased to have secretarial work done locally. Clubs and societies need people to prepare minutes, agendas, annual accounts, circulars, newsletters and so forth. Larger organisations often need someone to undertake temporary excess work or to fill in for an absent employee. You may be able to convince them that they would be better off using your services than employing a short-term 'temp'. You may be able to offer services to the general public, such as the presentation and production of curricula vitae and correspondence; writers' and drama groups, which can be found in virtually every town, often need someone to prepare their members' manuscripts and plays.

Your chances of success are obviously higher if you live in a town or city, within reasonable access of a college or university, and are within easy reach of the town centre. But don't despair if you live in a rural area. If you can provide a good service at a cheaper rate than people would have to pay for taking their business to the nearest town, you could be on to a winner. Word-processing has great potential as a service by mail too, and you could develop that aspect.

What will it involve?

Apart from brushing up your typing/WP skills (perhaps learning a new WP package) and acquiring essential start-up equipment, you will need to find out what demand there is for word-processing in your area and plan an appropriate marketing strategy. You will find information about start-up equipment needs in Chapters 1 and 6; Chapter 2 includes a section on assessing the market in your area and Chapter 5 offers advice on marketing your service.

Depending on your particular circumstances and aspirations, you may need to raise capital in order to purchase equipment and supplies, and you will need to organise an area in your home which you can use almost exclusively for your work.

There are also certain legal requirements you must fulfil, no matter how small your business, but these are relatively straightforward and should not cause any problems if you deal with them at the start. Chapter 3 provides comprehensive coverage of the formal aspects of starting a business and using your own home as a work base.

How far do you need to commit yourself?

The amount of time and effort involved in running a word-processing service really depends on how much *you* want to put in. The beauty of a home-based service is its flexibility, especially once you have built up a good supply of customers. It is possible to adjust your work-load to suit your own commitments and income needs. Your involvement and commitment can range from negligible outlay and a few hours' work per week in your own home right through to opening your own office services bureau with premises, staff and a full-time work-load.

There really are no hard and fast rules about how much of your time, effort and capital should go into your business, although you shouldn't expect to make a lot of money from it if you are not prepared to work regularly (sometimes at unsocial hours), meet deadlines and put in the effort required to keep good customers coming back. You *can* make money by working on a 'now and then' basis, but it will not be very much and it cannot be relied upon. If you want a more substantial, regular, income, then you must be prepared to put in considerable effort, especially in the first year when your business is becoming established.

Your chances of success

Every year, thousands of small businesses are started up and, sadly, an increasing proportion fail. In the case of home-based typing/WP services, the most common causes of failure include lack of preliminary research, inadequate and inappropriate advertising, insufficient forethought about the service offered and how the business will be run, and poor costing.

In addition, the price of WP equipment has fallen dramatically in recent years and many more people are now either trained or have taught themselves how to use it. These two factors mean that there is an increasing number of home-based (and office-based) businesses offering word-processing services and competition is rife! Unless the service you are offering is different, superior or more aggressively marketed than those of your competitors, your business may fail to achieve an adequate share of the market. Assessing the market and the competition, and developing a good business strategy, are therefore crucial to the success of a small word-processing service.

Another factor, often overlooked, is the level of enjoyment you get out of running your service. You will never make a great success out of any business if you are doing it solely for financial gain – you must *like* doing it. However, the most important factor is your own determination to succeed.

The first year is usually the most critical in terms of success or failure. Many services which might have developed into successful enterprises fail because their initiator loses heart at the lack of instantaneous success. Any business needs time to grow and develop and a word-processing service (especially a small or part-time concern) is no exception. The initial flush of enthusiasm in setting up the office and putting out a few advertisements may soon dwindle when results seem to be negligible. This stage is almost universal in business start-ups, but if you follow the advice given in this book and elsewhere and have the appropriate skills and personal attributes, there is no reason why *your* business should not be a success. Good luck!

Chapter 1
Look Before You Leap

This chapter aims to help you decide whether or not running a word-processing service is really for you. You probably wouldn't be reading this book if you didn't think it was, but before you skip straight on to Chapter 2, do at least consider some of the points raised.

Although setting up and running a word-processing service can be very rewarding, lucrative and interesting, *it is not easy*. The ability to type 60 words per minute and answer the telephone will not, on its own, enable you to run a successful word-processing service. You will need to have a confident, outgoing personality, and the ability to make decisions, meet deadlines and cope under stress. You will also need to be able to communicate well with people, both in person and on the telephone. Potential customers may be put off if you sound vague or unsure of yourself. Most important of all, you must be a self-starter. You will not have a boss or supervisor to tell you what to do. *You* will be your own boss. Don't make the mistake of expecting that your customers will treat you as an employee – they won't. The majority will expect you to take the lead in asking questions, ascertaining their precise needs, providing information, setting (or negotiating) deadlines and organising the actual work. So you must be able to make your own work-plan and stick to it. It will be up to you to decide how much work to take on, how much to charge, how long it will take to complete – and then actually sit down and get it done before your customer returns to collect it.

Are you the type?

Are you the sort of person who is going to cope well with, even thrive on, self-employment? The following self-assessment questions aim to help you to find out. Only *you* can know how realistically you answer these – there's no point in trying to fool yourself!

Don't be too put off if you feel inexperienced or unsure. Although running a word-processing service is very much like running any other small business, the risks involved are usually quite a lot lower. This is especially true if you are not the main breadwinner in the family and are not investing a large amount of capital. Under these circumstances, you can often afford to learn as you go along. You have relatively little to lose if you later find that it really is not for you. However, if you are more serious about making your service a success and if your success or failure is of some financial importance, *do* consider the following points very carefully before you decide to take the plunge.

Dealing with other people
How do you feel about other people in general? Do you usually enjoy meeting new people, or are you happier with people you know well and rather unsure of yourself with strangers?

Running a word-processing service usually involves a highly contrasted mix of working for hours on end on your own (or with your partner if you have one) interspersed with visits from customers (many of whom will quite happily spend hours of your valuable time chatting to you if you let them) and dealing with telephone calls. You will need to be very adaptable – happy to work alone for long periods and to interact cheerfully with your customers when necessary.

Adaptability
Are you generally easygoing, happy to accept the status quo and rather upset when changes occur, or are you eager for new challenges, ready to adapt and learn new skills?

If you plan to cater for the particular demand in your area, you will almost certainly have to learn new skills and/or adapt to seasonal changes. You will be working for many different people, all of whom will have very different ideas about how they want their work done. Unless you specialise, you will need to have, or acquire, the ability to deal with many different kinds of word-processing assignment.

You will also need the ability to switch off from one task at short notice and switch on to another. You will not be able to ascertain, or remember, the requirements of the new customer who has just arrived at your door with a batch of invoices for preparation if your thoughts are still at your desk constructing a CV for the previous one!

Industriousness and application
When you have a job to do, do you generally put it off until the last minute? Do you work well on routine tasks but find it difficult to

get on with more demanding jobs, or do you find you can't settle if you know you have something to do and feel a great satisfaction in doing the job well?

Running a word-processing service is like running any other business. If you don't produce the goods as required, your business will not last long. You must be able to apply yourself to the work you have taken on. Inevitably, some of it will seem either dreadfully routine and boring or so demanding it's difficult to know where to start. If you are normally able to set yourself goals in terms of getting work done, and almost always achieve these, you should have little difficulty.

Putting ideas into practice and making decisions

Are you generally unimaginative, preferring to follow the lead of others; occasionally inspired with a good idea but rarely bother to carry it out; or usually resourceful, inventive and able to put ideas into practice? Do you find it difficult to make decisions of your own and act on them? Perhaps you are happier to take orders than to give them?

One of the major factors affecting the success or failure of any small business is the ability to 'get moving', to put good ideas into practice. Having a good idea is not enough. You must be able to make it work.

You must also feel confident in your own ability to make and follow through your own decisions. If you are too easily put off, or diverted by other people's advice and criticism, you will never get your ideas off the ground. In addition, during the course of your work, you will often have to make rapid decisions: do you take on the extra work urgently required by the new customer who *may* provide a lot of regular work in the future and work overtime that evening in order to get it done; or do you turn him away because you have other commitments and feel your business can survive without his custom? Either way, the ability actually to *make* the decision, hopefully the right one, may be just as important as the decision itself. If you haver and dither, you will not only run the risk of putting your customer off for good, but of making the wrong decision (for you) as well. Planning in advance and having clear objectives (see below) will make day-to-day and long-term decision-making easier.

Planning, forecasting and organising

Are you poor at planning in advance, tending to make decisions on the spur of the moment when the need arises? Or are you a good organiser, far-sighted, able to plan in detail and then follow that plan through?

A major skill in the successful running of any small business is the ability to plan for both the long and short term. To begin with, your long-term goal may simply be to get your business off the ground but later, when your business begins to take off, you will find it easier to deal with problems such as work-overflow and the need for expansion if you have planned appropriately in advance. It is worth spending some time *before* you start up your business deciding what action you will take to achieve your aims. This means that you first have to *specify* your aims in terms of the financial reward required, the hours you wish to work per week, when you plan to take holidays and so on, and then decide how best you can achieve these goals. You will also need to be a good organiser, both of yourself and others, if you are effectively to plan your day-to-day work schedule and carry it out. You must be able to assign priorities to your work-load and decide on a daily plan of action.

Delegating and dealing with subordinates and colleagues

If your business grows, you may need to consider going into partnership, subcontracting or taking on staff. Therefore, the ability to organise and motivate others, as well as the ability to delegate responsibility, are also very important. Do you feel competent in dealing with subordinates? Can you give instructions with authority but without intimidation? Could you deal with unsavoury tasks such as disciplining staff or giving notice?

Determination and flexibility

When faced with a difficult task, do you tend to become disheartened if you can't achieve your aims quickly? Do you persevere for a while but find other things begin to take priority, or do you enjoy the challenge and almost always complete the task to your own satisfaction?

You will never achieve success with your word-processing service if, once you have set your goals, you do not have the will-power to plough ahead regardless of minor crises and problems. This does not mean that you must never reconsider or learn from your experiences. As well as the determination to succeed and the will-power to keep going under pressure, you must retain a flexible attitude which will allow you to change your plans in the light of new opportunities or altered circumstances.

Coping under stress

Running a word-processing service almost inevitably involves periods when you are overloaded with work and other times when you are barely ticking over. It is all too easy to underestimate the time required to complete a piece of work and, if you are working from home, the additional pressures/distractions of other commitments (family, friends, housework and so on) can cause great stress. Some of these aspects are considered under 'Running a business from home' later in this chapter.

Remember that most self-employed people necessarily work very hard, long hours and have to cope with the responsibility for the success or failure of their business 24 hours a day. Many people find it invigorating and inspiring to work under pressure whereas others find it extremely distressing. How do you cope with minor stresses? Are you inclined to make mountains out of molehills? Do you usually give up when things get too much for you, or are you generally able to see things in perspective, make an extra effort under pressure and cope well when the going gets tough?

Health and support

In addition to your personal attributes, you must be physically up to the task of running your own business. Is your state of health good enough to allow you to sustain the effort through difficult periods? Have you used a computer or word processor before: in particular, are you liable to eye-strain if you have to look at a screen for relatively long periods? People who suffer from epilepsy or migraine may find that operating certain VDUs aggravates their condition (this is because the screen 'flickers' – too fast for the eye to see).

Are your family behind you in your enterprise? You will find it very difficult to run your own business, especially from home, if your spouse has a negative attitude towards it. Make sure that you discuss your plans fully beforehand and that your family and friends understand the degree of commitment you must give to your business if it is to succeed. Consider how your family will be affected and explain to them any changes to routine which are likely to occur. Eliciting their co-operation and support may be essential to the success of your word-processing service.

Skills and abilities

The skills and abilities you need will, to some extent, be dictated by the kind of service you wish to offer. If you are going to set yourself up as a comprehensive word-processing/computerised data service for small businesses, you will obviously be using a different range of skills from those needed to operate a mobile secretarial service. Don't feel that you have to restrict your service to the expertise you already possess – be prepared to extend your skills and learn new techniques. After all, the wider the service you can offer, the more custom you are likely to attract.

There are certain skills you cannot do without, the ability to type accurately and reasonably fast being the obvious one. If you cannot type, or if it is some years since you did any typing and you need to brush up on your skills, there are several ways of reaching the necessary standard. Your local education authority will almost certainly run classes in your area, as may the Training Agency, and there are now numerous private agencies offering short, intensive courses in shorthand, typing and word-processing. Check in your local newspaper or enquire at your library for details.

If possible, give preference to a course that teaches touch-typing rather than one that requires you to look at the keyboard. You will be able to proceed faster and with fewer mistakes if you can acquire this skill. Touch-typing takes longer to learn but it is well worth it in terms of time saved later on. You should aim to achieve a typing speed of 50 words per minute (wpm) or more. Your course tutor or manual will tell you how to calculate your speed if you are unsure. Typing/word-processing is a very labour-intensive business, the cost of materials being much less than that of the labour input, so a significant proportion of your income per job is to cover the *time* you spend doing it (however you ultimately choose to charge). Therefore, if your typing speed is significantly slower than 50 wpm, you will either have to charge more and risk losing work to your competitors, or accept a lower rate of pay because you will be working longer hours for the same financial reward.

If you cannot attend a course, it *is* possible to teach yourself to type/word-process using a self-teaching manual (there are several available from bookshops and libraries and some are listed in Chapter 13). If you are purchasing a word processor or computer, you can use a typing-tutor program. This is a teaching system which runs on your computer or word processor giving instructions and monitoring your progress as you go. Iansyst Ltd produce two such programs: a 'crash course' for complete beginners and a 'two fingers to touch-typing' course for those already familiar with a keyboard. Both run on personal computers (PCs) and retail for £26.04 plus VAT. They can be purchased from Iansyst Limited, Omnibus Building, 41 North Road, London N7 9DP (071-607 5844).

You may also need to learn how to operate the WP package you have chosen for your business. All packages provide self-teaching manuals, some of which are easier to follow than others. In addition, some of the more advanced WP packages such as Wordstar, WordPerfect and Multimate are often taught as short courses by local agencies and colleges. You can also purchase VHS videotapes which claim to teach you to use some of these programs in a few hours, but these are rather expensive (eg the WordPerfect Technotape Video Tutor costs over £50). Some of the plethora of self-teaching books on these programs are listed in Chapter 13.

As well as the ability to type and use a word-processor, you will need a good understanding of grammar, punctuation and spelling. Many of your customers (business people and college students seem to be the worst culprits) will expect you to correct their mistakes. If your command of English is especially good, you could offer this as part of your service, although in general your customers will expect you to correct the odd spelling mistake as a matter of course. Spelling mistakes (and certain typing errors) are easily spotted if you have a WP package which includes a spell-checker. However, many of these use American rather than English spellings. This is rarely a problem nowadays as the two are often used interchangeably, but you may find some customers object to the use of Americanised spellings.

You will also need a fairly extensive knowledge of the various layouts and formats used in typing/word-processing. To some extent, this will depend on how much you intend to specialise. If you specialise, say, in preparing legal drafts, you will obviously need a very good understanding of the particular format involved whereas, if your service is more comprehensive, you will need a more general knowledge of how to lay out and present different kinds of material. Although some customers will tell you exactly how they want their work prepared, many will expect *you* to explain the various styles available and advise them on the most suitable for their needs. (Having some samples to show them is useful.) Examples of some basic layouts of various documents are included in the Appendix. Typing and word-processing manuals will give you a broader view of the variety of formats you could use.

Should you wish to extend your service beyond that of straightforward typing/word-processing, you will need to possess or acquire the relevant skills involved. Some of the additional services you might like to consider are outlined in Chapter 8. It is often the case that by offering a special service (such as an audio-typing facility for business men on the move) you can attract custom which would otherwise pass you by.

Finally, don't restrict yourself to the knowledge you already possess. Be prepared to learn new skills, at classes, at home, or even from your customers! If you can type, you can learn to operate a word processor; if you can do arithmetic, you can learn to do simple bookkeeping. The more skills you possess, the greater choice you will have in operating your service and the more customers you will be able to attract. You will also be able to charge more for your service if you can offer that little bit extra.

Running a business from home

There are a number of advantages and disadvantages in running a business from your home. Legal restrictions, the effects on rates and community charge, insurance, tax and so on are dealt with in Chapter 3. This section considers the other pros and cons of running a business from home.

The pros

Start-up costs are comparatively low and your income, relative to your outlay and hours of work, can be excellent (especially in comparison with other home-workers). By working for yourself, you'll gain a sense of accomplishment that you may not feel working for someone else. You can decide what hours you wish to work and you can fit your working hours around the care of children or other commitments which would make outside employment, or running your business from office premises, difficult. In addition, you save time and money which would be spent travelling to and from a workplace.

The cons

On the negative side, you may have to work long hours or at unsocial times (eg evenings and weekends): customers often seem to think that a home-based word-processing service should operate 24 hours a day. They would not expect this of an office-based agency.

You might also find it difficult to integrate your work with your social life. When you work from home, it is all too easy for family and friends to assume that your business is not very serious and to persist in interrupting you and/or expecting you to drop what you are doing and attend to them in a way they wouldn't even consider if you were an employee or ran your business from separate premises. You will need to be firm right from the start. Tell your family and friends what you are doing, explain what your working hours will be and let them know that you will not appreciate interruptions during those hours. You will need to prevent yourself from falling into the same trap. Working from home can provide many distractions and conflicts of interest: it can be difficult to settle down to a word-processing assignment when the washing up is sitting in the sink!

Essential start-up equipment

Assuming you will be starting your business from home, the start-up equipment you need will depend on the following:

(a) Where you will be doing your typing/word-processing.
(b) The kind of service you intend to offer.
(c) How much time you want to invest in your business.
(d) The income you require from it.

Your initial equipment will necessarily be geared to your aspirations of business success. While it might be rash to redecorate the spare room, invest in a brand new office desk, filing cabinet, dedicated word-processor, laser-jet printer and 20 reams of paper before you know there is an opening for your service, it would be equally unwise to start off with nothing but the family's battered manual typewriter and a few sheets of paper.

If you do start off with the minimum equipment in order to 'test the water', you should have a plan which will allow you to expand your business if it suddenly takes off. An office services work-load can build up incredibly fast and the last thing you want when you're just starting off is to lose customers because you haven't enough paper to complete a job or because your printer ribbon has run dry.

The bare minimum necessary to start a *typing* service includes a typewriter (preferably electric or electronic), a desk or table (with drawers) on which to do the work, a ream of good quality (85 g/m^2) A4 white typing paper and a small supply of envelopes, carbon paper, typewriter ribbons, pens, correction fluid (or ribbons), paper-clips and so on. If you are launching straight into a word-processing service, you will obviously need either a dedicated word processor or a computer with sufficient memory to run a reasonable word-processing program and a printer, as an alternative to the typewriter.

You should also purchase the necessary bookkeeping stationery (see Chapter 4) *before* you start your business: you will very quickly get into a muddle if you don't and besides, you'll want to keep a record of the supplies you've already invested in the business to offset against your income later on.

Although it is not *absolutely* essential, it is strongly recommended that you also have a telephone, a dictionary, a diary (both to make appointments for customers and to keep track of your hours worked) and some means of protecting and storing customers' work (a small supply of manilla folders and a drawer to keep them in will suffice).

A more comprehensive checklist of initial supplies is included in Chapter 6, which will also help you to decide on the kind of equipment which best suits your needs and how to acquire it.

Start-up costs

You may already own a portable typewriter and/or a home computer (not necessarily a PC) together with a cheap word-processing program and possibly a domestic quality dot-matrix printer. And you will almost certainly have a table or a desk on which to use this equipment. In this case (and assuming you are already on the phone and don't wish to invest much money to start with), you can start up your business for only a few pounds. Bear in mind, though, that a PC (or dedicated word processor) will not only support much better word-processing programs but will be much faster to operate. In addition, a very basic dot-matrix printer is unlikely to produce the print quality required by your customers and may not stand up to the rigours of business use.

Assuming you are buying equipment from scratch, you must first decide whether to go for a typewriter or a word processor. If you *really* want to go for a typewriter, consider a reconditioned second-hand model. These are generally much cheaper than new machines and usually just as reliable, but make sure that you get a guarantee. The price you pay can vary quite a lot: 1991 prices for *new* electric typewriters range from about £100 to £500, and for electronic models from about £150 to £600. The price variation is predominantly due to whether the model is compact or heavy duty and the range of features available. Expect to pay proportionately less for reconditioned models.

If you are prepared to pay a few hundred pounds for an electric typewriter, you should consider purchasing a word processor. These can be acquired (new) for under £400.

Other equipment can be purchased second-hand. *Don't* buy a new desk and filing cabinet while you are working from home (unless you would have bought them for yourself anyway); wait until you are making sufficient profit to expand into a business services agency! You should be able to acquire a good quality second-hand desk, filing cabinet and all your start-up supplies for under £200. A comfortable computer/typing chair, though not essential, would also be a good buy. A cheap new model will cost you about £20 whereas a good second-hand model may cost anything up to £80.

Initial start-up costs for a simple home-based word-processing service can therefore range anywhere between £20 and £1000 depending on how much equipment you already have and how much you want, or need, to buy.

One thing to beware of is being over-cautious initially. If you buy too cheaply to start with in order to avoid large losses in the event of your business failing, you risk losing money unnecessarily later on if you have to replace earlier purchases with more expensive equipment. Be realistic. If you intend to work full time at your business and hope to expand in the near future, then there is no point in buying a 'home' computer/word processor and cheap printer to start with. On the other hand, if you know from the outset that you will not be able to commit more than a few hours a week to the business and have no hope of expansion within the next few years, then it would be unwise to make expensive purchases of equipment initially – it will take you too long to recover the costs from your income. This is where forecasting and planning are essential. The next chapter will help you to formulate your business plan, an essential preliminary step. By the time you have done that, you should be in a position to decide whether or not to leap into the ranks of the self-employed!

Chapter 2
Planning Your Strategy

Having a clear idea of the potential market for your service, how much you are going to charge for it, what your costs will be and how you will attract custom are crucial to any preparatory plan. Your aim, armed with this knowledge, will be to provide a realistic forecast of the financial future of your venture. A well thought-out business plan will improve your chances of raising capital through your bank (if you need to) and provide a standard by which to measure the success of your service.

Many word-processing services are started up speculatively, without any preliminary research or financial plan: most of these are doomed to failure. Often, the service is priced too low in the hope of attracting custom, and with relatively high initial costs the venture appears to be a failure. At this stage, the service is often terminated on the assumption that the market is insufficient. A preliminary plan outlining initial and running costs, profit required, the input of working hours necessary to achieve this, sensibly calculated, and an estimated period by which profits should have reached the required level will allow the success or otherwise of the venture to be much more realistically determined.

Assessing the demand in your area

The first thing you must do is to find out what demand there is likely to be in your area (a look at Chapter 5 may be helpful here). To do this, you will need to find the answers to several questions.

Are there any office services agencies or home-based typing/word-processing services already operating in your area?
Most towns have at least one office services agency. These usually offer typing/word-processing, bookkeeping, telephone answering, an accommodation address, and printing and photocopying services to small businesses and private individuals. Temporary staff agencies may offer similar services. Office-based agencies will need to charge quite a lot more than you because their

overheads are much higher. Look them up in Yellow Pages, then phone them and find out what their rates are (most charge by the hour) and how long it would take them to prepare, say, a 20,000 word dissertation. (This will give you some idea of the work-load they have.) Find out what is included in their charge. Do they include a free copy? How much would they charge for extra copies? Is the work produced on a word processor or a typewriter? Will they charge extra if you want to make alterations later on?

Next, find out where the home-based typing/word-processing services are located. Home-typists usually advertise in the local press (under 'business services' or something similar), in shop windows, on university bulletin boards and so on. If there are home-typists advertising regularly in your area, you can be sure that there must be some demand for the kind of business you want to set up. Phone them up to find out their rates, how they charge, how fast their turnaround is and so on. It's probably not worth pretending to be a potential customer in this case - they will probably realise that you're not genuine anyway - and besides, you may find useful contacts this way. Explain that you are thinking about setting up your own word-processing service and are seeking advice from others in the same situation. They may be able to give you first-hand advice about running such a business locally. If there are other home-typists near you, perhaps you could arrange to pass on any excess work to each other. Customers are more likely to try again if, rather than simply saying you can't fit in their work at the time, you can helpfully pass them on to another typist who is not so busy.

Are there any clubs, charities, small organisations or societies in your area?

The best places to find a list of local societies and organisations are your library and town hall. Most boroughs produce an annual list (usually free). Sometimes the list is kept in the library for reference only (you will need to take a pen and paper to make a note of any likely addresses). Drama groups and writers' societies often need to have manuscripts prepared and other organisations need typed agendas, minutes, accounts, newsletters and so on. If there are many small societies in your vicinity, you may be able to attract business from them.

What higher educational establishments are there in your area?

Don't restrict yourself to your own town or village on this one. If you are lucky enough to live near a college or university, go in and enquire about the possibility of word-processing dissertations and theses. Typists advertise on the numerous notice boards in these establishments. Some colleges keep a list of potential dissertation typists in their central office. If you want to break into this market, you may be favoured if you can offer something special, such as correction of bad grammar/spelling/English, the ability to produce special scientific, mathematical or foreign language symbols, or a very fast turnaround. Students are notorious for wanting their dissertations typed up at the last minute!

Will you be able to attract small businesses which don't have their own secretarial staff and/or larger organisations with occasional work overloads?
The answer to this question really depends on the following:

(a) Where you are located relative to your potential customers.
(b) Whether you can attract trade with effective advertising (see Chapter 5).
(c) The extent of your own business training and office skills.

When my own service was first starting out, I was lucky enough to be able to attract work from several local large organisations for whom I had done 'temping' work in the past. (Beware of doing this while you are still officially working for the temporary staff agency. You will usually find your contract forbids it!) I also acquired steady work from several small businesses who could not afford staff of their own, but these contacts took several years to build up. The owners of small businesses rarely have the time to read advertisements and cannot usually afford to pay very much for 'secretarial services'.

In this area of the market more than any other, you will be expected to be entirely businesslike, competent and trustworthy. You must be able to convince your clients that you can do a thoroughly professional job at a much more economical rate than an office-based agency.

If you want to enter this market, you will probably need to consider whether you can offer any additional services which will attract customers, eg collection/delivery, on-site filing, telephone answering, photocopying, audio-typing, part-time work at your customer's premises, direct mailing and so on.

This is probably one of the most difficult markets to assess in advance. Sending out a mail shot to potential local businesses is probably the best way to probe this market. Advice on how to make the most of this approach is included in Chapter 5. You should be able to get a good idea of the number of small businesses in your vicinity from your Yellow Pages or Thomson directory; unfortunately, there is no way of knowing at this stage which of these might need outside secretarial help.

What opportunities are there for attracting business from the ordinary residents in your area?
This will depend on a variety of factors. The age structure, employment rate and population size will give you an indication of the number of people who are likely to need assistance with the production of a CV, for example; you will not be asked to type many of these if you live in a small village of predominantly retired people.

Apart from CVs, application forms and a few letters, ordinary individuals rarely require word-processing services, so this is not likely to be a very lucrative market on its own - you will need to attract business from other sources too.

Are there opportunities to offer a service through the mail?
Finally, don't think that you have to restrict yourself totally to the area in which you live. Many people are quite happy to send non-urgent material through the post if they hold a duplicate copy. If you advertise a particular postal service - perhaps in a specialist journal - you may be able to generate business from people outside your own area. This is particularly true if you can offer something extra, such as translation or a special knowledge of medical terms. My own business generated a reasonable income from the preparation and production of CVs by post and a colleague undertook the typing of essays for Open University (OU) students by advertising in the OU's nation-wide newsletter. Take a close look at your own skills: an ability you take for granted may be just what another person is looking for.

What kind of service will you operate?

Having made a preliminary assessment of the potential market in your area, you will need to consider whether your service can cater for any or all aspects of that market. What particular skills do you possess: are you confident of taking on any kind of assignment or do you wish to restrict your service to a particular field? In the initial stages, it's better to take on *any* word-processing work you can get. This will give you practice in tackling work you have perhaps never come across before, and it will also increase your knowledge of the market available, provide experience in dealing with different kinds of client and make more contacts for you. In this way, you will find out what you prefer to do and which assignments are the most lucrative and offer the most consistent work-load.

Don't worry if you've never seen a properly laid out CV, a dissertation or the minutes of a meeting before – you must expect to learn as you go along. Your service will attract more custom and will be more successful the more broadly based it is.

Once you have acquired a good regular supply of customers, you can begin to think about specialising. You will have an established business and plenty of experience to start from. If you choose to specialise, you need to be especially sure of your market. Many specialist home-typists work for only one or two big clients (perhaps doing overflow typing, envelope addressing or invoices). This can have advantages and disadvantages.

One WP operator, although working in a self-employed capacity, did virtually all her work from home for one large client. Things went well for a few years, the work was easy, she was not troubled with dealing with new customers or chasing up debtors, and the supply of work was well regulated to suit her requirements (though not particularly well paid). Unfortunately, when her client went out of business, so did she. Her client did not bother to inform her of the impending closure and she had no time to build up a supply of other customers to replace the lost income. Although this woman was not actually specialising in terms of the type of work she was equipped to do, the fact that she had limited her range of customers to such an extent had a similar effect.

You can specialise in terms of the kind of work you handle without necessarily restricting the number of clients you work for. If you can translate, index, summarise or understand technical jargon, you may be able to attract sufficient business from further afield to specialise in a particular type of work. However, unless you work primarily for a few established customers or your service is one which spreads by word of mouth, you may need to advertise almost continuously in trade journals or the press in order to generate enough business.

You might also like to consider related services such as bookkeeping, telephone answering and envelope addressing. This last occupation, however, has many pitfalls of which you should be aware. First and foremost, *never respond to an advertisement which asks you to send money*. You don't pay people to address envelopes for them, they pay you. Second, don't be misled by firms which provide advertising postcards but want *you* to pay for posting them (usually on a commission for sales basis). You are very unlikely to make more in commission than you pay in postage. There are, of course, respectable firms who *do* use envelope addressers but these firms rarely need to advertise.

Try writing to companies in your area which do mass mailings: clubs, large retailers and organisations. The firms which send *you* advertisements through the post are a good bet. Most of them pay a set, and rather low, rate for addressing a box of envelopes (which *they* provide). You should be paid more if you also fill, seal and stamp the envelopes.

How much time have you got?

Another factor you will need to consider is the amount of time you have available to devote to your service. For many small businesses, the hours of work are relatively fixed. Nobody wants their chimney swept at 10 pm or expects their local hairdressing salon to be open on Sunday afternoon. But this is not the case with a home-based typing/word-processing service. Unless you specify otherwise, you will find that many of your customers will expect you to be available in the evenings and at weekends. There is no reason why you should, of course, although offering a fast-turnaround service is a good way of attracting custom. Remember that your potential earnings will be limited by the number of hours you put into the business as well as your relative availability to customers (eg whether or not you are prepared to fit in an urgent piece of work even though this involves working unsocial hours).

Consider what hours you are prepared to work. Will these hours be fixed (say 9 am to 5 pm five days a week) or do you want to work on a more flexible time-scale? Will you be restricted to working entirely from home or will you be able, and willing, to work outside your home base?

Once you have decided how much you want to earn per week, you can calculate the number of hours you need to work in order to achieve this goal. Bear in mind that some of your time will be spent interviewing customers and answering enquiries, proof-reading, correcting mistakes, on the telephone, maintaining records, purchasing supplies and so on. You must make an allowance for this 'non-keyboarding' time when you estimate both the time required to complete a certain assignment and the rate you will charge. Make sure that your charges are sufficient to cover the number of hours you are putting into the business, not just those hours spent at the keyboard.

Your financial plan

By now, you have made an assessment of the market for a word-processing service, considered your ability to enter that market and decided how much time you are going to devote to your business. You are now in a position to draw up your business plan. This is basically a financial forecast in which you will be attempting to foresee the likely profits generated by your service based on the time, charges and expenses you estimate will be incurred.

Step 1. Decide how far ahead to plan. Although it may take some time for your word-processing service to start generating a good profit, you should not plan too far into the future. Make an assessment based on one year of business. You should be making a reasonable profit from your business before the end of your first year, since your initial expenses will be fairly low compared to other small businesses.

Step 2. Decide how much you expect to earn each month. To estimate this, you will need to work out what your charges are going to be – Chapter 4 will help you if you are unsure – and how much work you expect to generate. It is probably fairly realistic to assume that you will be working at your full capacity in six months' time. Estimate the progressive build up of work in the preceding months.

Step 3. Calculate the costs involved in providing this level of service. This will include all your expenses – paper, ribbons, electricity used, telephone calls, insurance, interest on loans to purchase equipment, depreciation of equipment, advertising costs and so on.

Step 4. By taking the costs and expenses from the total amount you expect to earn each month, you will be left with your net profit. You may find that this projects as a net loss for the first month or so, especially if you intend to purchase a lot of expensive equipment and to spend a relatively large amount on initial advertising.

Assuming all goes according to plan, this is the profit you can expect to make on your word-processing service. From it, you can decide whether your plan meets with your expectations, or whether you will need to modify it: for example, by increasing your charges. You will need to allow for the payment of National Insurance and income tax out of your net profit.

The following hypothetical plan for a home-based word-processing service is intended to assist you in producing your own forecast.

Jane Doe left work to start a family. Now her children are at school, she decides to start up a word-processing service – initially from home. She converts part of her spare bedroom into an office and, with her own savings, buys a PC, WP package and printer for £900 and other equipment (second-hand desk, bookkeeping requisites, stapler, files, storage disks and so on) for £150. These are assets of the business and don't appear on her financial forecast. She purchases a supply of paper, printer ribbons, envelopes and so forth. These are consumed as part of the service and are grouped under 'expenses'. She starts business in January. Depreciation on her resaleable equipment is estimated at £20 per month (see Chapter 4).

Jane ultimately expects to achieve a personal income of £5 per hour. Her charges will be slightly higher than this to allow for time spent interviewing, proof-reading and so on, and to cover her costs. Assuming she achieves a full work-load by June, she anticipates her service will be bringing in £980 per month. She intends to work seven hours a day, 20 days per month.

She estimates her total expenses for the year: advertising, printing business cards, telephone, postage, insurance, electricity, repairs and maintenance, direct costs (paper, envelopes, ribbons and so on). She then divides this figure by 12 to get a monthly figure.

From her financial plan, it is clear that Jane Doe's word-processing service is likely to be a success in the long term. But this plan is rather simplistic. First, costs incurred have been spread out over the whole year. In fact, most of the expenses would be concentrated in the first few months, especially advertising, ensuring adequate stocks of paper were available, printing of business cards and so on. If you want a more realistic month-by-month idea of cash flow, you will need to estimate the actual amount spent/earned each month. In addition, your bank manager would expect to see a breakdown of anticipated expenditure – and possibly income – if you were to apply for a loan or overdraft. Even so, according to this forecast Jane does

Month	J	F	M	A	M	J	J	A	S	O	N	D
Anticipated income	50	100	300	500	850	980	980	980	980	980	980	980
Anticipated expenses	200	200	200	200	200	200	200	200	200	200	200	200
Depreciation	20	20	20	20	20	20	20	20	20	20	20	20
Profit (loss)												
- per month	(170)	(120)	80	280	630	760	760	760	760	760	760	760
- cumulative	(170)	(290)	(210)	70	700	1460	2200	2980	3740	4500	5260	6020

Simplified financial forecast for Jane Doe's word-processing service

not make any real profit until April. If her costs had been distributed more realistically, she might have expected to run at a loss for four months or more.

Second, her forecast does not include the cost of paying herself a salary or drawing money from the business. For the first few months, she would only be able to draw a salary, or indeed cover her costs, by having an overdraft, loan or using personal savings. A more detailed cash flow forecast planner is provided as an appendix to 'Starting and Running Your Own Business' available free from the Small Firms Service.

If Jane Doe had not made a financial forecast, she might well have dissolved her word-processing service after three or four months because her business appeared to be a failure. By preparing a financial plan, she can see the future potential of her service and whether or not her business is following the expected trend, and hence whether her original estimates were accurate or need revision.

Going it alone or in partnership?

The Jane Doe example is based on one type of business structure – that of the sole trader. The majority of home-based word-processing services start off on this basis and it is the simplest form of business management. If you wish to operate as a sole trader and intend to run the service under your own name, there are no legal formalities – you simply inform the Inland Revenue and the Department of Social Security (DSS) that you have begun trading. (See Chapter 3 if you intend to use a business name.) One of the disadvantages of sole trading is that there is no distinction in law between the owner and the business. The debts and obligations of the business are regarded as those of the owner. Consequently, creditors may make claims on your personal estate for any debts owed to them by your business. On the other hand, because owner and business are one, any profit made belongs to the proprietor (but is subject to income tax). Another possible disadvantage of sole trading is that you lack the support of colleagues (and their help), and so you need to have expertise in a number of areas.

Alternatively, you may know one or more other people who are interested in starting up a word-processing service. By pooling capital, labour and skills, you may be able to operate a more successful business than if you opted to go it alone. A partnership can be started without any legal formalities if you trade under the surnames of all the partners (though again the Inland

Revenue and DSS need to be informed), and can comprise up to 20 proprietors.

Although it is not a legal necessity, it is advisable to have a formal agreement between the partners drawn up by a solicitor. This is called a Deed of Partnership: it states the liabilities of each partner and the percentage of profit to which each partner is entitled. A deed will prevent any quarrels about who owns what or who is entitled to what and should limit the extent of your liability if your partner signs a contract or enters into a business agreement which is financially disastrous. If you don't do this, the provisions of the Partnership Act 1890 will apply. (The legal status of a partnership is different in Scotland from that in the rest of the UK.) See also Chapter 9, page 152, on partnerships.

As for sole traders, partners are responsible for the debts incurred by the business and all are entitled to a share of the profits. One important point worth emphasising is that *all* partners are responsible for the debts of the business. This means that if your partner makes a rash purchase and then disappears, the suppliers can turn to you for payment. The same applies to income tax. If your partner fails to pay income tax on his share of the profits, the Inland Revenue can ask *you* to pay it.

Great care should be exercised in the choice of partners. Many partnerships go wrong because disputes and disagreements occur which had not been foreseen – going into partnership with someone can ruin a perfectly good friendship. Pick partners who are committed and responsible. If they have skills and abilities which complement your own, you will both benefit more from the partnership than if you pick someone with similar abilities. Partnerships *can* work, but they are often problematical.

The principle disadvantage of the sole trader or the partnership lies in the fact that the owner(s) carry an unlimited liability for the debts and obligations of the business. This can be overcome by forming a private limited liability company. This is a separate legal entity for which you can work as an employee (as well as being a director). Word-processing services do not usually operate in this way, although it may be worth considering when your business reaches the stage of expanding into a business services agency or secretarial bureau. A company can sue and be sued just like a person and any monies to be paid must come from the company funds and not from the pockets of the directors. A company must have at least two shareholders, one director and a company secretary (who could be a second director). These people don't necessarily need to 'work' for the business.

Setting up a limited company from scratch is a complicated (and costly) matter. Seek the advice of your bank manager or accountant if you are considering this possibility. An alternative is to buy a limited company as a 'package' from one of the firms which specialise in producing these ready-made companies. My own firm was formed in this way and I found it to be a quick, relatively cheap and uncomplicated way of setting up a company.

A limited company is bound by much stricter legal requirements and constraints than a sole trader or partnership. For example, a limited company must hold an annual general meeting of shareholders and make an annual financial return to the Registrar of Companies. Also, there must be a registered office (the specialist firm which sells the package may offer an address for the registered office, or your accountant may take on the address).

Unfortunately, most creditors, including banks and equipment hire firms, still require personal guarantees from the directors of 'new' companies. You may not be any more protected by forming a limited company than you would be operating as a sole trader or partnership.

Chapter 3
Starting Your Business

For many people, the actual setting up of their business seems to be the most difficult stage in the whole operation. Don't be put off by the necessary, but sometimes rather daunting, red tape involved. The legal requirements are really very simple (assuming you have elected to operate as a sole trader or partnership) and you should have little difficulty if you follow the advice given here.

Legal requirements – people you need to inform

Anyone can start up a business, trading under their own name without any legal formalities whatsoever. You can employ staff and buy or lease property and equipment in connection with the business.

However many hours you work in your business and whether or not you are also in paid employment, you must inform your local Inspector of Taxes within a few days of commencing your word-processing service. His address appears in the local telephone directory under 'Inland Revenue'. You will probably be asked to complete form 41G which asks for basic particulars of yourself, your business and your previous employment. If you have given up paid employment to start up your word-processing service, your local Inspector of Taxes may also require your P45 (a form detailing your income and tax paid which should be given to you by your employer when you leave).

You should also inform your local DSS office. Do this before you actually start your service otherwise you could lose any entitlement you may have to be exempted from paying National Insurance contributions (see Chapter 4).

Your home

Community charge, rates and planning permission
Rates on personal domestic dwellings have now disappeared and been replaced by the community charge. When residential property was subjected to rating assessments, the local rating

office produced a special assessment which rated the property for business and domestic use, depending on the proportion of the property used for business purposes, and the business rates could form the basis of a tax claim. You will not receive any reduction on the community charge, even if you decide to convert half of your house into an office. However, you *may* incur an additional business rate. The rating authorities still consider the nature and extent of the business in determining whether a business rate will be charged. If you convert your front room into an office services bureau and erect a large sign outside, you may well have to pay business rates (in addition to the full community charge) and you would also require planning permission for such an extensive change of use. If, however, you make only minor alterations to your premises – for example, converting part of a spare room into an office – you are not obliged to inform the rates department nor obtain planning permission, and your rates should not be affected. If in doubt, contact your local rates department and ask.

Planning permission is usually only required for fairly extensive, or obvious, changes of use to the premises. A word-processing service is usually fairly discrete; it should not require alteration to the premises, erection of signs or other obvious indications that your home now incorporates an office. You will not normally need to apply for planning permission unless you are making extensive changes such as these.

If you rent rather than own your home, check the terms of your tenancy agreement. Although most tenancy agreements preclude the use of the premises for business purposes, they do not normally forbid the operation of a small part-time business such as a word-processing service, provided that it does not disturb other tenants, attract a business rating assessment for part of the premises or require alteration to the building. It is probably wise to inform your landlord that you intend to do occasional word-processing work from home and ask for his confirmation that this is in order. He may look on this more favourably than if he finds out through the grapevine that you are carrying on a small business from his premises without his knowledge!

It is also wise to check the deeds if you own your house or flat, because they may contain a covenant specifically excluding business use.

Capital gains tax

The advantage of setting aside part of your home primarily for the use of your word-processing service is that you can claim a proportion of heating/lighting and so on for tax relief under Schedule D (see Chapter 4). The drawback is that the Inland Revenue may levy capital gains tax on the proportion of the profit from the sale of your home equal to the proportion of the premises used for your work. They are entitled to do this even if you subsequently sell the property as being solely for domestic use. Sometimes the revenue authority is not concerned when only a tiny proportion of the home is used for business purposes, but if there is a considerable sum to be realised (and this may happen if your home increases rapidly in value and you have used, say, a third of it solely for your business) then a demand will be forthcoming.

However, capital gains tax is only payable if there is *exclusive* business use of the room(s). You can usually avoid it by ensuring that your 'office' is also used for domestic purposes from time to time, as a spare bedroom for guests maybe, or a place for the children to do their homework.

In addition, you are allowed to make capital gains of £5000 (1990-91) in each year before you are liable to pay capital gains tax. (Since independent taxation was introduced in April 1990, both husband and wife are entitled to £5000 exemption. If you run your service as a partnership with your husband, you could make £10,000 on the sale of the portion of your home used for your word-processing service and still not have to pay capital gains tax.)

Neighbours
Neighbours are another potential problem depending on the district in which you live and the type of premises you occupy. Consider carefully whether your word-processing service will cause any inconvenience or annoyance to them. If you expect most of your clients to visit you, are you sure that there is sufficient room for them to park their cars for short periods without causing an obstruction? Will clients have to use a shared access to reach your premises? Will the noise of your typing or your printer disturb anyone? (This is especially relevant to people living in flats, or if you intend to work late into the evening or at weekends.)

The best way of avoiding problems is to inform your immediate neighbours in advance of your intentions, and take a reasonable attitude to any complaints raised. You should be able to reduce any problems caused by noise by sensible location of your office, and the use of mats and covers or 'quiet' machines. If parking or access is likely to be a problem, you can either ask that your clients visit only during certain hours (for example, when you know your neighbours are likely to be out) or ensure that they park their cars at an appropriate place.

Choosing and using a business name

Although the majority of home-based word-processing services operate under the name of the owner, there are advantages to be had from using a business name. Your advertising may have more impact and people may remember your service better if you have a catchy business name – hence, you may generate more business than you would if you operated under your own name. Also, the use of a business name may add an element of professionalism to your service which may also attract more custom. Finally, if your service is a great success and you eventually want to set up in a separate office, you can take your (already well-known) business name with you and so ensure that your established customers know where you have gone.

It is no longer necessary for business names to be registered (except in the case of a limited company). There are, however, restrictions on permissible names and a requirement to comply with the regulations. Details are available from the Registrar of Companies. You cannot, for example, use the same business name as another business in the same field or a confusingly similar name, and your business name must not give the impression that it is connected with Her Majesty's government or any local authority. Hence, you are not allowed to use words such as Crown, King, Queen, Prince, British and so on.

The best way to ensure that you are complying with this is to look up similar agencies operating in your area and make sure that you are not using one of their business names (or a very similar one). Also, make sure that you don't use the name of any well-known agencies even if they don't have a branch in your area. (It is possible that you will choose a name that is being used by another small word-processing service elsewhere in the country; however, it is very unlikely to seek an injunction against you for misleading people into thinking your business is the same one!)

To comply with the terms of the Companies Act 1981, the directors of a business must:

- state their names and addresses on all business stationery;
- display in a prominent place on the business premises a notice containing their names and addresses;

- give their names and addresses in writing to any business contact who asks for their information.

These regulations should not cause any significant problems. You should simply include your name and address and those of your partner(s) on your business stationery, business cards, invoices and so on. You don't need to divulge this information in an advertisement, although you will probably want to include at least your telephone number. The regulation about displaying a business name on your premises is not really intended for a business run from the owner's home (since it's relatively easy for your clients to find out who you are and they already know where you live!), but you can put up a notice in your 'office' area, or wherever you normally interview your clients, stating the name of your business together with your name and address.

So the legal requirements are fairly straightforward. Actually choosing a suitable business name is not necessarily so easy. Ideally, you should choose a name that not only 'sounds' like the kind of service you intend to operate but is also easy to remember. You can use real words - for example, 'Perfect Print' or 'Smiths Office Services' - or make up new words which sound appropriate - for example, 'Wizzword'. Try to think of a name that gives the right impression of your particular service. Perhaps you are offering a very high quality business service with a guarantee of accuracy. You will want to convey the sense of quality, service and accuracy in your business name - something like 'Top Flight Typing' or 'Exec-U-type' might be appropriate. If you are offering a fast-turnaround word-processing service, you may want to emphasise other aspects - perhaps 'Wizzword' would be appropriate here, or 'Fast Fingers'. If you are totally stuck, it might help to write down all the features of your service that you feel are important or special. Next, list all the words you can think of that relate to those features and then try combinations of those words and part words. You should come up with several 'catchy' sounding names. Now all you need to do is to decide which one you are going to use for your word-processing service.

Bookkeeping

However small your word-processing service, you should keep full and accurate records of all your takings and expenditures in relation to the business right from the start. Not only will the Inspector of Taxes require an accurate statement of your profits (he is entitled to estimate your profits if you cannot supply an accurate record) but you will soon lose track of the progress of your business, and may also have difficulty in chasing up non-paying clients or tracing purchases, if you do not maintain a sensible record system. This subject is dealt with in greater detail in Chapter 4.

Insurance

Even while you are working from home, you will need to have adequate insurance to cover loss or damage to your business equipment or large amounts of stock. You should also ensure that you are covered against claims by your customers should they sustain any loss or injury while on your premises (public liability insurance). This is often covered in a general business policy. If you are not taking out a separate policy, you should check whether 'business' customers are covered by the provisions of your household policy.

You must also have employer's liability insurance, by law, if you employ another person (even a spouse), and you may wish to consider personal insurance for yourself and possibly other insurances (eg loss of earnings cover) if your income from the business is crucial.

While working from home, your normal household contents policy should be sufficient to protect you against the loss of inexpensive items such as your pocket calculator. However, you may need to make special arrangements for more valuable items such as a word processor, printer, photocopier, telephone answering machine, mobile phone and so on.

You should check the terms of your household contents policy carefully. Such policies are devised for private dwellings – if you are regularly visited by clients, you may be required to pay a higher premium. If in doubt, write to your insurance company informing it that you will be running a small, word-processing service from your home and asking whether or not this will affect your contents policy. Unless you plan to purchase a lot of expensive equipment and run a fairly substantial business, you will probably find that your general contents insurance premium will not be increased.

If you plan to use your car extensively for business purposes (perhaps by operating a mobile secretarial service or a collection/delivery service), you will also need to ensure that your car insurance policy will cover you while you are officially working.

Insurance is a complicated business and it would be sensible to consult an insurance broker, whose services are free of charge to clients (they receive a commission from insurance companies). Your insurance broker will tell you what insurance is necessary for your particular requirements and will shop around for the best deal for you. Most reputable brokers are members of the British Insurance Brokers' Association, 14 Bevis Marks, London EC3A 7NT (071-623 9043). Further information about insurance and the use of brokers can be found in Chapter 10.

Help and advice for new businesses

Perhaps the first sources people think of when seeking advice on setting up a new business are the bank manager, solicitor and accountant. The advice of your bank manager will probably be free but you will normally have to pay for advice from your solicitor or accountant. Unless you are starting off with something bigger than a one-man operated home-based word-processing service – say a partnership, on separate premises, or with a small staff – you are not likely to need the professional advice of a solicitor or accountant at this stage, although you may need to consult your bank manager if you wish to borrow money to buy equipment.

A number of organisations now specialise in offering advice and information to small businesses. The Small Firms Service, which is run by the Department of Employment, provides a nation-wide counselling service to owners of small businesses, including home-based word-processing services, and has regional centres throughout England. The responsibilities of the Small Firms Service will pass to Training and Enterprise Councils (TECs) as they emerge. In Scotland, the Small Firms Service is operated through the Scottish Development Agency and in Wales through the Welsh Development Agency. A similar service is provided in Northern Ireland through the Department of Economic Development (see Chapter 12 for addresses).

The Small Firms Service can be contacted most easily by telephone on 0800 222999 (Freephone Enterprise). You will be put in touch with a professional business counsellor who will be able to offer free advice on all aspects of setting up and running a small business. Alternatively, you can write to the Small Firms Division of the Department of Employment. As well as direct consultations, the Small Firms Service also produces a range of free leaflets which provide useful general information on setting up a business, basic bookkeeping, marketing, employing staff and so on (see Chapter 13).

The Rural Development Commission (which now incorporates CoSIRA – the Council for Development in Rural Areas) offers a similar service for small businesses in English rural areas. It produces a comprehensive guide entitled 'Action for Rural Enterprise' giving advice and information on finance, premises and marketing. The booklet can be obtained from its head office or one of its regional centres. Much of the advice relates to the tourist trade but some is of a more general nature. You can contact the Rural Development Commission at 141 Castle Street, Salisbury, Wiltshire, SP1 3TP (0722 336255) and you will be put in touch with your nearest regional centre. In rural Wales, a similar service is offered by the Development Board for Rural Wales, Ladywell House, Newton, Powys SY16 1JB (0686 626965) and in Scotland by the Highlands and Islands Development Board, Bridge House, 20 Bridge Street, Inverness IV1 1QR (0463 234171) and the Scottish Development Agency, 120 Bothwell Street, Glasgow G2 7JP (041-248 2700).

In addition, there are now numerous enterprise agencies which offer free advice and information to local small businesses. These agencies are usually founded by an association of industry, commerce, educational establishments and the public sector, to assist and encourage economic growth in the area. Your local authority will be able to provide a list of useful agencies and contacts.

Chapter 4
Money Matters: Finance and Accounting

Raising money

Assuming you start up your word-processing service using your own home as a base, you should not require a great deal of capital to purchase the necessary equipment. Later on, when your business has grown and you wish to move into separate premises and acquire more equipment, you will possibly need to raise more finance.

The cheapest way to finance your business is to use your own money – personal savings, redundancy money, saleable assets (jewellery/antiques) and so forth. If you do not have sufficient personal funds, there are several ways in which you can raise money to purchase your initial equipment.

Loans and overdrafts

A loan is perhaps the most obvious way of raising money. You may have friends or relatives who will either lend you money directly or guarantee a bank overdraft, or loan, on your behalf. Your bank will probably be willing to provide you with either an overdraft facility for several months or a direct loan – especially if you are an established customer – but it will want to see a business plan showing your setting-up costs, expected income, fixed and variable costs, and overheads. Your business plan should also include information on the nature of the business you propose to run, the potential market, your qualifications and experience, staffing and equipment arrangements, and so on. Most banks have specially prepared 'business plan packages' to help you with this. In addition, the manager may well look for some form of security before agreeing to give you a loan. Many sole traders use their home, or occasionally valuable personal possessions, as collateral. (See also Chapter 10 on the government's loan guarantee scheme.)

The advantage of an overdraft is that interest (usually two to three per cent above base lending rate) is only paid on the actual amount by which you are overdrawn; the disadvantage is that it can be called in at any time. Overdrafts are usually agreed for only one year, with a review thereafter, whereas loans are more generally for two to five years. You can claim tax relief on bank charges and loan interest related to your word-processing service.

The four 'big' banks (Barclays, Lloyds, Midland and NatWest) all have special schemes for new small business customers including loans and overdraft facilities. Some provide free banking for 12 months and all supply a helpful package of booklets covering the difficult areas, in addition to recommending publications to buy.

There are also numerous private finance agencies who may be prepared to give you a loan, but their interest rates are often very high. If you are considering using a private financier, consult your solicitor.

Grants
You may also qualify for a grant. Local authorities and agencies throughout the country have schemes to encourage and aid new businesses. In Berkshire, for example, the County Council provides start-up grants of up to £1000 to new co-operatives and grants of up to £500 to young people aged 16 to 25 to help defray the costs of starting up their own business. Most other local authorities operate similar schemes so it is well worth enquiring.

Hire purchase and leasing
Most office equipment can be acquired by either hire purchase or leasing and this is often a good alternative to taking out a loan to purchase equipment outright. If you are considering hire purchase, check how much you will be paying over and above the direct sales price, and that the equipment eventually becomes your property. You may be able to get a better deal (pay less interest) by getting a loan and buying outright. Leasing equipment is a very good idea for a word-processing service. If you lease your word processor, photocopier etc, you will pay a monthly rental and the equipment remains the property of the lessor. The major disadvantage of this is that you never ultimately own the equipment and you can neither sell it or use it as collateral for any other type of borrowing. On the other hand, you will normally be provided with an in-built maintenance agreement, a facility for rapid replacement if your machine breaks down and the option to upgrade your equipment as and when necessary.

Enterprise Allowance Scheme

The Enterprise Allowance Scheme, set up by the government, is designed for those receiving unemployment benefit who would otherwise lose this income if they started up their own business. Full details of the scheme can be obtained from Jobcentres and your local Training and Enterprise Council. Basically, it provides successful applicants with £40 per week for up to a year to offset the loss of unemployment benefit and to give their business time to 'get off the ground'. Once you have started your business, even if you obtain revenue from customers, the £40 is guaranteed so it can be banked.

Any kind of business venture will be considered - I know of several home-based word-processing services started up under this scheme. To qualify, you must be over 18 but under retirement age, you must have been receiving unemployment benefit (or under a notice of redundancy) for at least eight weeks and you must show that you are prepared to invest £1000 in your business as a sign of good faith. This does not have to be in cash; you might already have equipment or a bank overdraft facility to this amount, for example. There is considerable demand for the scheme and you may have to wait some time to set up your business. You must not start up your business before your application has been approved. Further information can be obtained from Jobcentres or by dialling 0800 222999.

A business bank account

You should seriously consider opening a separate bank account solely for your word-processing service as soon as you start operating your business. Although it is possible to use your own personal bank account (and you will almost certainly need some kind of bank account as many customers will want to pay by cheque), keeping track of the monies entering and leaving the account which are related to your service can become quite a headache. If your word-processing service is very small and your income from it very low, you should have few problems in using your personal bank account. If, however, you hope to expand your business in the future and/or receive a good income from it, then you should open a separate bank account at the outset.

Apart from making it easier for you to keep track of your word-processing profits, having a separate business bank account will also be an advantage if you need to dispute any tax assessments imposed by the Inland Revenue. It is much easier for you to prove your income and outgoings if your service has its own bank account than if you have to attempt to separate your word-processing service banking from your personal banking.

Keeping records

While your business is still relatively small, you will probably not require the full range of accounts books normally used by businesses, although you will need to acquire these if your business expands. You can purchase the various types of account books at stationery shops or buy a ready-made small business package. Kalamazoo, for example, produce a package called 'Bookkeeper' which is aimed at the small business. It is divided into sections and includes provisions for VAT, a cash book and petty cash book, journal and ledger, cash flow forecast and trial balance. Easy-to-read instructions are given at the beginning of each section. 'Bookkeeper' costs £14.95 (plus £3.50 for postage) and can be ordered from Kalamazoo plc, Customer Service Department, Mill Lane, Northfield, Birmingham B31 2RW (021-411 2345).

If you are operating as a sole trader, do not employ staff and operate a system whereby you pay for purchases (such as paper supplies) immediately and your clients pay for their work on delivery, you should be able to manage reasonably well with a simple cash-book system. You may prefer to have two cash books if you have a business bank account: one for recording cash receipts and their payment into the bank and all withdrawals by cheque, standing order or direct debit, and the other for recording payments into or out of the float of loose cash kept at your workplace.

Alternatively, if you invoice your customers for payment at a later date and/or you yourself obtain goods or services on credit, you will need to have separate books (called sales and purchases day books) for recording the amounts owing to you (debtors) and the amounts owed by you (creditors). You will need these figures for your own information and for the preparation of your final accounts. In addition to your basic accounts book(s), you should have some means of securing or filing copies of invoices generated by yourself and receipts for purchases made in connection with the business. A filing cabinet is ideal but two large ring binders will work just as well initially.

Bookkeeping is a chore to most small businesses but it has to be done. It is absolutely essential to keep proper and accurate records right from the start. If you are absolutely hopeless at figures, then you should consider hiring a bookkeeper to set up your records system and to maintain interim checks to see that all is well. Many accountants and bookkeepers are self-employed and work from home (just like yourself). You should find a good selection in the 'Business Services' section of your local newspaper or in your Thomson directory or Yellow Pages. Their rates will be more reasonable than those of a large agency or group of accountants. You can also get a useful free leaflet from the Small Firms Service entitled 'Accounting for a Small Firm' by D F Millar.

You need to keep sensible and accurate records for two reasons. First, you will need records from which to extract your annual accounts and to make assessments of your profits for VAT, National Insurance and tax purposes. Second, your records will provide valuable information *to you* on the performance of your word-processing service, allowing you to see where purchasing or costing policies need to be reviewed and efficiency improved.

If you are running a computer, you may wish to keep your accounts on it. There are many suitable software packages.

The cash book

This is your most essential book (and perhaps the only one you will need initially). You can purchase a good quality cash book from any stationer or office supplier. It should have columns in which to insert the following (minimum) information: date, details of the receipt/payment, amount received/paid, and a column for inserting any folio/reference of your own (for example, the invoice/receipt number or purchase number; this will allow you to locate the separately filed receipts, invoices and vouchers referred to in the cash book).

In your cash book, you will record your receipts on the left-hand side of a double-page spread and any payments you make on the right (see figure opposite). You can use the same book for both cash and cheque receipts and payments. You should update your cash book every day and it is a good idea to start a new double-page spread every month and total up your receipts and payments at the end of each month. Your first entries will almost certainly be on the 'payments' side; don't forget to include the purchase of your cash book as a payment!

Debtors

If you provide work on credit terms for a few customers, you can easily keep track of outstanding accounts by filing unpaid copy invoices in a ring binder. Check these every week to make sure that your customers are not taking too long to pay you – you may

RECEIPTS				PAYMENTS			
Date	Detail	Ref	Amount	Date	Detail	Ref	Amount
1991	Brought forward		402.00	1991	Brought forward		130.16
3/2	A. SMITH	102	40.00	4/2	PRINTERS LTD	26	14.28
5/2	B. JONES	103	13.50	10/2	STATIONERS LTD	27	36.12
6/2	S.M. LITTLE	104	24.00	21/2	POST OFFICE	28	10.50
12/2	M. BOOTH	105	58.60				
15/2	J.R. CLIFFE	106	2.50				
20/2	L. GRANGE	107	104.60				

Sample cash book

need to send out reminders or statements. When your customers pay you, bank the money, enter the receipt in the cash book and place the invoice in the file of paid invoices.

Creditors

As with sales invoices, if you have only a few purchase invoices each month, files for unpaid bills and paid bills will work reasonably well. When you actually pay the bill, write it on the payments side of your cash book and move the invoice from the unpaid file to the paid file. Two useful booklets dealing with the handling of debtors and creditors are available from the Small Firms Service. They are 'Trade Credit' and 'Prompt Payment Please'.

Sales and purchases day books and ledgers

If you issue a large number of sales invoices (most of your customers pay you at a later date) and/or regularly defer payments, you may eventually need a sales day book in which to keep a record of invoices issued, when and to whom, and a purchase day book giving details of your suppliers and the amounts owed.

The ledger sets out details, taken from the sales and purchases day books, of individual customers' and suppliers' accounts and serves as a record of amounts owed and owing.

Value added tax

It is very unlikely that your turnover will be above the compulsory VAT registration level (£25,400 in 1990-91) while you are a sole trader working from home, but if it is you will have to keep *separate* records of the VAT you pay and the VAT you charge to your customers. This is not as complicated as is generally believed, especially if you keep your records up to date on a daily basis. You will either need to keep separate books to show VAT paid and received or have additional columns in your cash books (and journals) in which to separate VAT from the total receipts and payments. More about VAT on page 62.

Employees

If you employ staff, you will need to keep records of their pay, tax and National Insurance. You will not necessarily need a wages book for this since the Inland Revenue will send you a copious supply of forms (including sheets for recording wages and deductions for each employee) when you tell them you are taking on staff. You will be responsible for deducting tax from your employees' pay at source under the PAYE scheme and you will also be required to pay both the employer's and your employees' Class 1 National Insurance contributions to the Inland Revenue each month (though you do, of course, deduct the employees' contributions from their earnings).

Your local tax office will provide all the necessary forms and advise you how to do this. They provide a special starter pack for new employers which is very comprehensive and fairly simple to follow.

Annual accounts

The Inspector of Taxes will require you to send financial information relating to your service each year in order to assess your taxable profit. From 6 April 1990, you need not send detailed accounts to your tax office if your turnover is less than £10,000. You just send them your turnover figure, expenses total and net profit. However, you will obviously need to compile the details for your own use to arrive at the figures.

You are not obliged to engage an accountant to prepare your accounts (unless you form a limited company). Having said that, if, after reading this section, you are at all unsure about the presentation and layout of annual accounts, you should consider engaging an experienced bookkeeper or an accountant to prepare them for you. Many bookkeepers are able to produce accounts, and a self-employed bookkeeper may be able to prepare your accounts at a fraction of the fee charged by an accountant. If you intend to do this, you should make doubly sure that your daily records are adequate – this will help to reduce the fee you have to pay.

If you engage an accountant, the Inspector of Taxes will normally deal directly with him rather than with you. Tax returns and formal notices of assessment of tax, however, will be sent direct to you.

The date to which you make up your accounts is entirely for you to decide. Form 41G (from the Inland Revenue) requires you to specify your proposed accounting date, so you will need to decide this when you start your business. Pick a date that will be convenient for you – perhaps the end of your first year of trading, or the calendar year end, 31 December, or even the end of the tax year, 5 April. Once you have chosen your accounting date, you should make up your accounts to that date each year and submit them to your local Inspector of Taxes.

Annual accounts are usually in two parts: the profit and loss account (which summarises the year's transactions) and the balance sheet (which shows the assets and liabilities of your word-processing service at the chosen accounting date).

Preparing your profit and loss account

Your profit and loss account will show your gross profit, or how much money you have actually received, on the right-hand side and your expenses, usually broken down into sections, on the left-hand side. Your net profit (or loss) is then shown as the difference between these two figures. The following example should make these points clearer:

Profit and loss account of Susan Smith
(trading as Smiths Secretarial Services)
for the year ended 5 April 199_

		£	£
Gross income from work done			10,638.00
Less:	Depreciation	420.00	
	Advertising	531.25	
	Stationery and supplies	792.50	
	Printing (business cards)	25.00	
	Postage	41.00	
	Telephone	125.45	
	Electricity	102.00	2,037.20
NET PROFIT			8,600.80

Note. In this example, Susan Smith's turnover exceeds £10,000 and she will therefore have to submit her accounts in this detailed form to the Inspector of Taxes.

In assessing the expenses for heating and lighting used in relation to your business, it is conventional to apportion your actual electricity/gas bill on the basis of the proportion of your home used primarily for running your word-processing service. If you have a six-roomed house and use one room primarily for your business for example, you could claim up to one-sixth of your heating/lighting bill as a business expense. It is probably better if you try to maintain an accurate record of the telephone calls you make in connection with your business – you can claim the cost of these as a business expense.

Remember to include *all* your expenses. If you use your car (for example, to collect and deliver work), then you should claim for the petrol used. If you have to pay an additional premium on your house insurance because you work from home, include this as an expense. You should also include any wages paid to your employees (and related contributions), interest on business loans or overdrafts, any professional fees you pay and depreciation (see later).

Balance sheet of Susan Smith
(trading as Smiths Secretarial Services)
as at 5 April 199_

	£	£
Fixed Assets		
Computer (Amstrad PC2286/40)	1,000.00	
less depreciation	250.00	750.00
Printer (HP Laser-jet II)	600.00	
less depreciation	150.00	450.00
Desk	80.00	
less depreciation	20.00	60.00
Current Assets		
Sundry debtors		102.85
Balance at bank		450.00
TOTAL ASSETS		1,812.85
Capital		500.00
add Net profit (for year)	8,600.80	
less Drawings	7,489.95	1,110.85
Sundry creditors		202.00
TOTAL LIABILITIES		1,812.85

Your balance sheet shows the state of affairs of your service at a particular date.

You cannot claim your own self-employed Class 2 National Insurance contributions (or income tax) as an 'expense', nor should you include any solely personal or domestic expenses.

Preparing your balance sheet
Your balance sheet is a record of the money (capital) you have invested in the business, the value of your fixed assets (word processor, printer, photocopier etc) and current assets (balance at bank), and any liabilities you have (loan, creditors). A simple example is shown on page 56.

Depreciation
Depreciation is an estimate of the reduction in value of your fixed assets (including premises, which usually increase in value) over the year. There are several methods of estimating depreciation, the commonest being the 'straight-line method'. By this method, you estimate the useful life of the asset and its residual value (how much it will be worth) at the end of that time, and then divide the amount to be written off by the end of the estimated life, giving a fixed amount of depreciation each year.

Example

A word processsor is purchased for	£450.00
Residual value estimated at	£ 70.00
Leaving (to be written off)	£380.00

Estimated life = 7 years
Annual depreciation = £380.00 ÷ 7 = £54

In the profit and loss account shown on page 55, depreciation on the fixed assets of the word-processing service is taken to be 25 per cent of the reducing balance per annum. The computer, for example, purchased for £1000.00 is considered to have a resaleable value of £750.00 after the first year of use and £562.50 after the second year.

Although you will show depreciation in your profit and loss account and it reduces your net profit (and therefore your 'income' from your business), depreciation is not allowable against income tax and you will have to account for it in your tax return (see Income Tax section later). Capital expenditure (eg buying a hard disk drive for your PC) is treated in the same way. However, you can claim 'capital allowances' on these items (see below).

Capital and revenue

An important convention is the separation of 'capital' and 'revenue' expenditure. Revenue expenditure is the day-to-day running costs of the services and is included in your profit and loss account; capital expenditure is that with which 'assets' are purchased (eg a new printer) and this is shown in your balance sheet and is *not* debited as an expense in your profit and loss account. It is not always easy to make the distinction. Clearly, a computer is a capital item and the cost of repairs to it is revenue expenditure, but what about a new disk drive? Usually, common sense is the best guide in making such distinctions. Note, however, that capital expenditure is eventually paid for out of revenue: the computer is written off in the profit and loss account.

Drawings

Many self-employed people think that they pay tax only on what they take out of the business for themselves as 'drawings' or 'wages'. This is not so. Drawings are sums taken on account of the profit you expect to make. You are taxed on your *total* net profit before deducting any drawings (see the section on tax computation on page 61).

Income tax

Everyone is entitled to earn some money without paying tax on it. This is currently (1990-91) £3005 per annum with an additional £1720 being allowed to a married man (this allowance can be transferred to his wife if he has insufficient income to use it all). For those over 65 years of age, the personal and married couple allowances are higher and there are additional allowances for those with disabilities, one-parent families and so on. So, if you are a single woman under the age of 65, £3005 is the amount you can earn (your net profit) before you are liable to pay income tax. Assuming you do not have any other income, then you will have to pay tax on any profit you make in excess of £3005. If you are also in employment and pay tax through a PAYE scheme, then you will probably be liable to pay income tax on the whole of your word-processing service profit because your personal allowance will have been taken into account in your employment.

Self-employed people do not pay tax through PAYE: this method of collecting tax is strictly for employees. Instead, they pay tax on their profits under what is called a 'Schedule D' tax assessment.

At present, there are two rates of income tax. The basic rate is 25 per cent and applies to the first £20,700 of taxable income (ie income after deduction of any personal and special allowances). The higher rate is 40 per cent, which is levied on taxable income above £20,700 per annum.

If your profits are likely to exceed your personal allowance (or if you are in paid employment in addition to running your word-processing service), you should take care to put money aside for tax later on. You may be charged interest on overdue tax, so it is in your best interests to have the money available for payment at the appropriate times. If you are in doubt, your local tax office should be able to advise you.

National Insurance

There are four classes of National Insurance (NI) contribution. Briefly, these are:

Class 1. Paid by people who work for an employer and who pay tax under the PAYE system.

Class 2. Flat-rate contributions paid by *self-employed* people.

Class 3. Voluntary contributions for people not liable for either Class 1 or Class 2 contributions.

Class 4. Graduated contributions paid by *self-employed* people with earnings between certain limits.

If you are employed and wish to run your word-processing service in your spare time, you may be liable for both Class 1 *and* Class 2 (and possibly Class 4) contributions. Your employer will arrange for the payment of your Class 1 contributions but you must arrange for the payment of any other contributions. You may be liable for additional Class 1 contributions under certain circumstances. Leaflet NP28 issued by the DSS gives further details. If you are not employed elsewhere, then you may be liable to pay Class 2 and possibly also Class 4 contributions, depending on how much profit you make.

Class 2 contributions are paid weekly either by direct debit from your bank account or by stamping a contribution card, which the DSS will send you on request, with stamps bought weekly from a post office. The current (1990–91) rate of Class 2 contribution is £4.55 per week.

In addition, you may be liable to pay a Class 4 contribution based on your profits chargeable to tax after deducting any capital allowances. Fifty per cent of a self-employed person's Class 4 contribution is allowable for income tax relief in calculating taxable income. Currently (1990-91), Class 4 contributions of 6.3 per cent are levied on profits between £5450 and £18,200. The section on tax computation (page 61) shows how to calculate capital allowances, profits chargeable to tax and Class 4 income tax relief. Leaflet IR24 (Inland Revenue) explains how profits are assessed for Class 4 contributions, and leaflets NI41 and NP18 give details of the rates of Class 4 contributions and the age limits of contributors.

Exemption from paying National Insurance contributions

You will be *exempt* from paying National Insurance contributions if:

1. you are over retirement age or under 16, or
2. you are entitled to reduced contribution liability as a married woman or widow (you must have exercised your option not to pay Class 2 contributions before 11 May 1977), or
3. your earnings from your word-processing service are below the small-earnings limit (£2600 per annum in 1990-91).

In order to be exempt from Class 2 contributions, you must apply for a 'Certificate of Exception' from your local DSS office (ask for leaflets NI27A and CF11). You are automatically exempted if you are incapacitated for work.

Normally, your profits from the previous year are used in assessing your eligibility for exception from Class 2 payments. However, if in your first year of trading, you expect to make less than the small-earnings limit, you can still apply for exception. Your DSS will expect you to provide evidence to support your claim, so you will have to show that you have made a reasonable estimate of your likely earnings. In subsequent years, the DSS will require a copy of your annual accounts if you wish to have your exception certificate extended.

Although it is a good idea to avoid paying National Insurance contributions unnecessarily, especially if your business is very small or takes a long time to build up, your entitlement to the benefits afforded by National Insurance may be affected. If you are concerned about your entitlement to any National Insurance benefits (pension, sickness benefit, maternity allowance etc), you should ask your local DSS office for advice before you decide to apply for exception. You can get advice by dialling 0800 666555.

What to send the tax inspector

You will need to send a copy of your accounts (detailed as explained earlier if your turnover exceeds £10,000) together with a 'tax computation' to the Inspector of Taxes each tax year. Susan Smith's tax computation is shown below and an explanation of how she arrived at the figures follows.

Susan Smith
Profit adjusted for income tax
Year ended 5 April 199_

	£	£
Profit per accounts		8,600.80
add Items not allowable for tax purposes		
less depreciation		420.00
		9,020.80
less Capital allowances	420.00	
less private use of fixed assets	105.00	315.00
TAXABLE PROFIT		8,705.80

Tax and National Insurance calculation

Taxable profit		8,705.80
Deduct: Class 4 NI (50%)		102.56
		8,603.24
Deduct: Personal allowance		3,005.00
TAXABLE INCOME		5,598.24
Total income tax payable: 25% × £5,598.24		1,399.56
Class 4 NI payable: £8,705.80 less £5,450.00 at 6.3%		205.12
TOTAL		1,604.68

(Payable in two equal instalments of £802.34)

Depreciation, capital expenditure and capital allowance

Susan's first profit figure is taken from her profit and loss account (see page 55). Since depreciation is included in this figure, and is not a deductible expense against income tax, she has to add the depreciation figure from her profit and loss account to her net profit. However, she *is* allowed to claim this as a capital allowance.

Capital allowances are to cover that part of your profits you should be setting aside for the replacement of those assets which either become worn out or obsolete. In this particular example, Susan estimates that her fixed assets (ie computer, printer and desk) are used privately by the family about a quarter of the time. Thus, she has to deduct 25 per cent from her capital allowances before adding this on to produce her new 'taxable profit' figure. As you can see, this is higher than the net profit figure from her accounts because it allows for the fact that she is deriving *personal* benefit from her business's assets. The same situation might apply to the use of a car which is used partially by the business and partially for private use. Capital allowances on the depreciation need to be apportioned between private and business use.

Tax and National Insurance computation
Next, Susan computes her tax and National Insurance payable. She starts off with her taxable profit figure. Since this is between the Class 4 contribution limits (£5450 and £18,200), she must pay Class 4 contributions. These will be £8705.80 (her taxable profit) less £5450.00 × 6.3 per cent, which she calculates as £205.12.

She is allowed income tax relief on 50 per cent of her Class 4 contributions (£102.56 in this example), which she deducts from her taxable profit. She then deducts her personal allowance and works out the tax payable on the remainder of her income. She adds her Class 4 contribution payable to this figure to find out how much she has to pay to the Inland Revenue.

Paying tax and NI contributions
Tax and Class 4 contributions on the profits of your word-processing service will usually be paid in two equal instalments on 1 January and 1 July. Some time after you send in your annual accounts and your own tax computation, the Inspector of Taxes will send you a notice of assessment telling you how much you will be required to pay and when.

Value added tax

Compulsory registration
If your taxable turnover – that is, the amount of money your service earns per annum rather than your net profit – exceeds a

certain amount (£25,400 in 1990-91), you must register with your local VAT office (you can find it in the telephone directory under 'HM Customs and Excise') and charge VAT at 15 per cent to your customers. This tax is paid by you to Customs and Excise. It is unlikely that your business will reach this level of turnover while you are working single-handed from home, although you should keep an eye on your income and notify the VAT office if your turnover looks likely to reach the compulsory registration figure.

Voluntary registration
You can apply for voluntary registration if your taxable turnover is below the compulsory registration limit, but you will have to satisfy Customs and Excise that you have a 'compelling and continuous business need for registration'.

Advantages of being registered
The advantage of being registered is that you can offset the VAT you will have to pay for supplies and equipment against the VAT you will be able to charge your customers. If you receive more VAT than you pay, the difference has to be paid to Customs and Excise. If you pay more VAT than you receive, you can reclaim the difference.

Disadvantages of being registered
The disadvantages are:

(a) Your customers will have to pay more than they would if you were not registered.
(b) You will have to keep accurate and separate records of all VAT paid and charged, as well as completing a VAT return every three months and having visits by VAT officers.
(c) You will normally have to remain registered for two years from the date of issue of your VAT registration certificate (even if your registration was voluntary).
(d) The regulations governing what is 'standard rated' and what is 'zero rated' or 'exempt' is rather complex. You would have to charge VAT at 15 per cent on an individual letter, for example, but if you produced an A4 leaflet and provided 50 copies of it, VAT would be 0 per cent (zero rated).

Further advice about VAT
If you think you might need to (or prefer to) register for VAT, you should get advice from your local VAT office. It can also provide

several free leaflets, among which 'Should I Be Registered for VAT?', 'The Ins and Outs of VAT', 'Printed and Similar Matter' and 'Keeping Records and Accounts' are particularly useful.

Changes in income tax, National Insurance and VAT

The figures quoted here are correct at the time of going to press (1990-91). However, personal allowances, National Insurance contribution rates, lower earnings limits and VAT registration limits, among other things, are reviewed annually and announced in the Budget. You should check the current rates with the appropriate authorities.

Pensions

It may seem a bit pre-emptive to ask you to consider your pension (state or personal) at this stage but it is a matter to which you should give some thought if you are seriously intent on becoming self-employed.

How much you will get from the state when you retire depends on the National Insurance contributions you have made throughout your working life. DSS leaflet NP32 'Your Retirement Pension' gives full details of contribution requirements and the types of pension now available. Basically, the number of qualifying years of National Insurance contributions made during your working life determines what, if any, state pension you are entitled to. Important points that you may need to consider are:

- If you are a married woman and you elected to pay a reduced rate of National Insurance contribution, you may not be able to claim a pension of your own on the basis of these contributions. Your pension would be linked to your husband's contributions.
- If you are the recipient of child benefit, or have to stay at home to look after a dependant, you will be protected (for those years) by 'home responsibilities protection'. This means that those years will be automatically deducted from the number of years required to qualify for a full pension, instead of showing a gap in your record.
- If you are granted a 'certificate of exception' from paying National Insurance contributions on the grounds of small earnings (and you do not have 'home responsibilities protection' described above), your National Insurance

record will not be credited during any period of exception and you may find your retirement pension reduced as a result.

The DSS will provide a written statement of your projected state retirement pension based on your current National Insurance record on request.

You may also want to consider a personal pension plan, especially if you are the main earner in the family. If you are in employment and run your word-processing service on a spare-time basis, you may belong to an occupational pension scheme. However, if you are not in an occupational pension scheme, you should consider one of the multitude of plans and policies available for the self-employed. Your insurance broker will be able to provide details of a number of different schemes and advise you on the most appropriate for your needs.

Pricing, costing and estimating

The financial plan you devised earlier (see Chapter 2) should have given you an insight into your initial and recurring costs, and provided a broad view of your anticipated earnings over several months. How are you going to convert that broad plan into the day-to-day costing of assignments?

Methods of charging

One of the first things you will have to decide is *how* to charge for your service. There are a number of conventional methods of charging which depend as much on personal preference as on the type of assignment, and there is no reason why you shouldn't adopt several methods depending on the circumstances and your customers' requirements.

Many word-processing services and most secretarial agencies charge an hourly rate. If you do this, your customers will expect you to give them an estimate of the time it will take you to complete an assignment. You should take into account the complexity of the work (are there a lot of tables; is the language very technical?) and the way in which it is presented to you (is the handwriting very bad; will you be expected to reword it?) when estimating the time it will take you to complete it.

Almost all home-typists initially *under*estimate the time it will take to complete an assignment. Until you are more experienced and can produce fairly accurate estimates, you should think about doubling your first estimate. Your customers will be happier (and more likely to use you again) if your estimates are realistic, or even too high, than if they suddenly find themselves being charged twice as much as they expected because the assignment took longer than you anticipated.

For straightforward typing/word-processing that is easy to read, it should take you about one hour to type roughly 2000–3000 words (depending on your typing speed). You can estimate the number of words by counting the number of words on one (typical looking) line, then multiplying by the number of lines per page times the number of pages. Add extra time if the writing is difficult to read, if there are tables or lots of tabulations involved, or if you have to correct spelling and grammar as you go along. Remember to allow time for proof-reading at the end, and perhaps for correcting any mistakes you make, as well as for any special requirements such as making photocopies, ruling up tables (if your word-processor does not do this), stapling, providing envelopes and so on. Finally, if you are charging by the hour, you will need some method of accurately recording the time spent working on a particular assignment.

Another popular method of charging is per page (this normally means per A4 page). You can operate a sliding system of charges depending on whether your customer wants double-line or single-line spacing and whether each page comprises only a small amount of text (say a short invoice) or is completely filled (a newsletter, for example). Again, you will need to be able to estimate how many pages a particular assignment is going to cover. This will depend on the customer's requiremements, the point size and typeface of your word processor/printer, and the margin settings you use. A good way of finding out how much text you can get on a page is to print out a few pages in single-line and double-line spacing, as well as a few small sample invoices and letters; time yourself while you are doing this so that you can see how long particular assignments take you. If your word processor/printer supports a range of founts, it might be worth running off a variety of samples. You should then be able to estimate how many pages of text will be produced by a particular assignment and provide your customer with a reasonably accurate idea of what the final charge will be.

Charging by the number of words (usually per 1000 or part thereof) is another useful method. One advantage of this method is that the onus is on your customer to make his own estimate of the likely charge (if he wants to know what the assignment will cost, he can count the number of words himself). On the other hand, if you are not using a word processor (which will calculate the number of words for you), *you* will have to count (or estimate) the number of words in the assignment in order to charge your customer. Another problem is that this method is not very appropriate for small assignments such as the odd letter or a small batch of invoices where the number of words might never reach 1000. In these circumstances, you could use your rate per 1000 as a *minimum* charge per job.

You can, of course, have a combined charging system. Dissertations, theses, and manuscripts, for example, can usefully be charged per 1000 words (the student or author concerned will normally have a good idea of the number of words: dissertations usually come to between 8000 and 20,000 words; masters' and PhD theses up to about 80,000). Letters, invoices, leaflets and so on could be charged per page or by the hour. CVs could be charged per job; that is, a set charge covering the interview, construction of the CV, word-processing and printing, binding and producing a certain number of copies.

Another method which can be effective if you are working regularly for several small businesses (or taking in regular overflow work from larger firms) is to charge a set quarterly retaining fee and then a reduced hourly rate when any work is required. In this way, the business concerned knows that it has 'retained' your services and that you will be available to deal with any work as and when required. In addition, *you* are provided with a regular income in the form of the retaining fee. The disadvantage of this method is that you lose some of the potential flexibility that comes with a home-based word-processing service. Once you have accepted a retaining fee, you must be prepared to take on work from that business source as and when it is provided and attend to it very promptly. You can't decide to turn away work for a week while you decorate the house or go on holiday!

What will you charge?

The amount you actually charge will be a balance between your costs (and the time you put in) and the going rate for word-processing services in your area. You should have a good idea of what rates are being charged in your area if you followed the advice in Chapter 2. You should also ask yourself several other questions. How do the charges of other services relate to the quality/type of service being offered? Are the services that are charging a higher rate offering a better service? How do other services compare with the one you are offering?

In addition, if you are adopting several methods of charging, you will need to ensure that your rates per hour, per 1000 words and per page tally reasonably well; that is, you are charging roughly the same price for a dissertation whether you charged your hourly rate, your rate per 1000 words or your rate per page. You can check this when you do a long piece of word-processing by timing yourself and then comparing this with your rates per 1000 words and per page.

Bearing in mind that office-based agencies invariably charge more than home-based services and that rates vary according to the area in which the service operates, hourly rates of between £4 and £10 are typical for home-based word-processing services and £6–£15 per hour for office-based agencies. These rates are for straight typing/word-processing. If you are offering additional services, charge more.

One common fault with many home-based word-processing services is undercharging. While there may be advantages in launching your service with special cut-price rates in order to attract custom, there is no point in running a business that does not make money! Because most types of 'home work' (especially for women) are still grossly underpaid, it is all too easy to feel that your service is not worth very much to your customers. If you want to work 10 hours a day for £1.75 per hour that is entirely up to you – you may be able to attract custom with such low prices but you may also become quickly disheartened with your business if it provides such negligible financial rewards. Don't assume either that undercharging will necessarily bring you more customers. Statistics show that people are very wary of excessively low prices, equating them with lack of quality, poor goods and shoddy service.

If you charge a little more than other word-processing services near you but have a more professional attitude and dedication to your service than your competitors, you will soon find customers queuing at your door and you will be reaping the rewards, both financial and psychological, of a properly run business.

Chapter 5
Sell Yourself! Marketing Your Service

Even a very small business should give some thought to 'marketing'. This is not the same as 'selling' – selling is only part of marketing. Other important aspects are knowing your market and forecasting (see Chapter 2), and pricing, costing and estimating (see Chapter 4).

Advertising

Effective advertising is important for almost any business but it is especially crucial for a home-based word-processing service. You may be offering the best service in the country but if no one knows where you are, or what you can do, your business will never be a success.

Advertising serves two purposes: to bring your service to the attention of your customers and to persuade them to use it. You will therefore need to use appropriate advertising methods in order to maximise both the number of potential customers who will find out about your service and the number who will be convinced that it is worth using.

Free promotion

Unfortunately, advertising is often quite expensive. However, there are many ways of getting your message across without actually spending any money!

Many local newspapers and radio stations are interested in new businesses starting up in the area and may be happy to do an item on your service. The same is true of specialist magazines and journals who may be willing to insert a small editorial notice informing their readers that you have set up a word-processing service of special relevance to them.

Your Thomson directory will be happy to give you a free insertion in both its classified and alphabetical sections (as well as some free stickers and leaflets telling people that you can be found in Thomson's). You can also have a more prominent advertisement providing details of the kind of service you are offering but you will be charged for this. Yellow Pages has a similar system, but will only allow a free entry for subscribers with a separate business telephone number. Again, you must pay for a more eye-catching advertisement. Details of whom to contact regarding insertions can be found in the relevant directory.

If you are planning to type dissertations, theses, essays, book manuscripts and so forth, a good method of 'free' advertising is to put up leaflets on the notice boards in colleges and universities near you. It is also worth leaving details of your service – neatly printed on an index card – with the administration office of these establishments as many students, staff and even members of the public will contact the college or university office to enquire about typing/word-processing services in the area.

Careful planning and construction should go into your notice. Don't simply scribble your name and address on a scrap of paper and pin it on the board under 'Typists'. Prepare your notice neatly and perfectly and make sure that you include all the relevant details and information about the service you are offering. Highlight special promotional features such as 'rapid turnaround', 'free copies', 'translations', 'correction of spelling and grammar', 'scientific and mathematical symbols available', plus any specialist terminology you understand. Use a bold heading to attract attention and don't forget to leave clear details of how and when you can be contacted. A pocket containing a supply of your cards or tear-off strips with your telephone number on are a good idea. You can 'perforate' these quite well with a dressmaker's wheel. It is probably worthwhile stating your rates – many students don't want the bother of telephoning several typists to compare rates and services, so if your advertisement gives all the details they need and clearly states your policy on corrections and alterations (which can be fairly common in theses), you should be able to attract a lot of custom from this quarter.

Another possible source of free advertising is to use the free notice boards provided by large stores and supermarkets. Some of these specify that 'trade' notices are not allowed but many will permit you to pin up one of your business cards or a small index card giving details of your services. This is a good way of promoting services that are of interest to the general public such as a CV or letter writing service.

Shop window and post office notice boards
Putting up notices in shop windows and sub-post offices is a fairly cheap method of advertising. Most shops charge about

10p–30p per week to display a notice in their window. Again, think carefully about *what* you are going to say on your notice and *which* shops will be the best to use. In general, people hardly ever need personal typing or secretarial services, but if you can put up notices near business or university areas, you may be able to attract attention to your service for very little outlay. Town centre printing and copying shops, office suppliers and stationers may also allow you to put up a notice on their premises for a small charge. You may be able to convince a print and copy shop to promote your business by agreeing to have all your copying and printing done there.

Classified advertising

Advertising under the 'Business Services' section of your local newspaper is often a very effective method of attracting business. Many people – business men, students, writers and so on – look for typing/word-processing services in the classified ads section. This can seem expensive, especially at first when your business has not really started to cover its costs, but a regular advertisement is often the most effective method of promoting a word-processing service. Most local newspapers offer a sliding scale of charges with reductions (or free insertions) if advertisements are run for more than one or two days. Don't make the mistake of advertising once a week for a month and then deciding that this method is useless because you have acquired hardly any customers! You will have much greater success if you run an ad every day for three months. This will be expensive but it has been shown that this kind of advertising needs to be frequent and long term in order to achieve results.

I proved this to myself by running an advertisement twice a week for four weeks to which very little response was received (in fact, the business generated through this advertisement didn't even cover the cost of advertising), followed by the same advertisement every day for two weeks. At the end of the fortnight, I was so inundated with work that I had to subcontract it to another word-processing service!

The wording of classified advertisements is even more crucial than that of notices because you need to get your message across in a much more economical way. A large boxed advertisement will attract more attention and is often useful at the beginning of your promotion. Use it again intermittently to remind people about your service. You can follow this with a smaller, regular, two- or three-line advertisement which will be much cheaper to run. The wording of your advertisement should be positive, in short sentences, and should stress the professionalism and quality of your service. The two following examples show how economy of words and a positive approach can produce a much better advertisement for the same cost.

Example 1
Do you have typing or word-processing requirements? Experienced typist offers external secretarial services. Tel: Mrs S Smith (0101) 343434.

Example 2
TYPING & WORD-PROCESSING. Speed and accuracy guaranteed. Collection and delivery, free copy, reasonable rates. Tel: Susie (0101) 343434 (24 hours).

If you are offering a special service, make sure that your advertisement appears in the appropriate classified section. People looking for a change of job will notice a CV production service advertised under 'Professional Vacancies', for example, while hopeless letter writers may notice an ad in the 'Personal Services' column.

A very specialised service (such as medical or legal word-processing) could be advertised effectively in an appropriate professional journal. Most of these have a classified advertisement section but their rates vary considerably. Contact the classified section of the journal to ascertain its charges.

Many areas of the country also have a free weekly advertising paper (often delivered to every household) which will carry your ad. The rates are usually very reasonable and your freesheet may have a greater circulation than the local daily newspaper.

Nation-wide daily newspapers are another possible channel for classified advertising, but their rates are generally *very* much higher than those of local papers. If you are offering a service that can usefully be operated through the postal system, then nation-wide advertising could be a good idea. Again, you will need to advertise regularly and for an extended period in order to achieve results. Because this form of advertising is relatively expensive, you want to be fairly sure of recouping the cost through the business you generate from it. *BRAD* (*British Rate and Data*), a monthly publication which you should be able to obtain from your reference library, carries an exhaustive list of publications, advertising rates and circulation statistics. *Willings Press Guide* and *Benn's Press Directory* provide even larger lists.

For further advice on constructing good advertisements and marketing you could try *Successful Marketing for the Small Business* by Dave Patten, 2nd edition, (Kogan Page) which provides a comprehensive coverage of all types of advertising for the small business and *Marketing* which is issued free by the Small Firms Service.

Direct mail

If you want to encourage small businesses to use your service, a direct mail shot can be an effective way of targeting potential customers. Unfortunately, the typical response for mail shots is usually fairly low. Only about 2-5 per cent of the people you contact are likely to show an interest in your service which means that fairly large mailings are usually necessary.

You can either produce a suitable leaflet yourself and copy it or have a batch printed professionally (this will be more expensive, of course, but should look more impressive). As with your notices and advertisements, the leaflet you send out directly to small businesses should be well laid out and concise. Find out which local businesses are likely to need your services (their advertisements in the local paper, Thomson directory and/or Yellow Pages will help) and make a list of these. If possible, find out the name of the owner and address the mail shot to him personally using the mail-merge facility on your word processor.

Remember to keep your message short and to the point. Managers of small businesses do not have the time to read through pages of print, so keep the text down to one side of a small leaflet (say one A5 sheet). They are also likely to throw your leaflet straight into the bin after reading it, regardless of whether they might want to use your services later, so give them some incentive to keep the leaflet (eg print a complimentary calendar on the back of it), or enclose one of your business cards (which is more likely to be kept for future reference), or even an easily completed reply-paid postcard which they can send off to receive further information or arrange an interview.

Emphasise the speed, accuracy, reliability and confidentiality of your service. Pin-point the features which are likely to be of interest to small businesses, such as audio-typing, telephone dictation, collection and delivery, on-site filing and so on. Consider whether you could offer a more comprehensive service, for example a computer database facility for storing the records of a small business, bookkeeping or wages preparation. Perhaps you are willing to work at your customers' premises for some of the time or would be prepared to 'fill-in' during holidays or sick leave.

It can also be fruitful to follow up a mail shot with a phone call a day or two later. This reminds the contact of your service and gives you the opportunity to discuss his particular needs in relation to the service you can offer.

When mailing local groups, enclose your business card (several for a writers' society) and phone them the following week to ask if they would like to know any more about your service.

The major cost of a large-scale mail shot is likely to be postage. Delivering your leaflets by hand will alleviate this cost but it is usually only feasible if you have a fairly small area to cover and plenty of time in which to do it. Remember that while you are out delivering leaflets, you are not in to answer the telephone. You can benefit from special post office rates for bulk deliveries (2000 items or more) if you pre-sort (by postcode) your leaflets. Contact the business services department of your central post office for further details.

Word of mouth recommendation

The benefits of 'word of mouth' recommendation are incalculable. Most small businesses know others, writers know other writers, unemployed people needing CVs know others needing CVs, students wanting dissertations prepared know others in the same situation. If you provide a good service, the chances are that your customers will tell other people about it and you will receive a lot of 'free' publicity and custom in this way.

Of course, you can also receive 'bad' publicity if your service is slow, if you make a lot of errors or if you are unfriendly. You should be aware of the importance of your reputation locally. A few shoddy assignments, a week of disorganisation because your word processor has broken down and you have no back-up or a grossly over-priced dissertation can set back your business. Not only will your customer not return with further work but he will also probably advise others not to use your service.

'Blowing your own trumpet' can also be very effective. Tell people about your service. Get them to pass on details to their friends or likely clients. Ask your customers how they came to find out about you. Do they know anyone else who might be interested in your service? Could you give them a leaflet for their friend?

Business cards

No matter how small your word-processing service, a batch of properly printed business cards is well worth the investment. Not only can you enclose these with direct mail shots and contact letters but you can also leave supplies at your local copy-shop, further education establishment, writers' society and so on, as well as handing them out liberally to anyone and everyone. Carry several with you so that you can pin them up whenever a suitable notice board presents itself or hand one out whenever someone mentions the need for a typist.

Your business card needs to be attractive and informative. Try to indicate the range of your services without cramming too much on to the card. Your name, business name and telephone number are the obvious essentials. You may also like to include your address and a brief description of your service. For example:

SUSIE'S SECRETARIAL SERVICES
Word processing, typing, computerised bookkeeping, fax and copying

Dissertations	Manuscripts
Business	Personal
Reasonable Rates	Rapid Turnaround

Contact: Susie Smith
1 Any Street
ANYTOWN

Tel: 0101 343434
Fax: 0101 343535

Most printers produce business cards. Ask to see some samples. They will help to formulate your ideas for your own business card. Try to get several quotations before deciding which printer to use – their rates can vary. You should be able to get an initial batch of 100 cards printed for about £20–£35 with a discount for batches of 500, 1000 or more. Additional discounts may be possible if you have headed stationery printed at the same time.

It is probably a waste of money to have letterheads, invoices and other stationery printed while you are still operating your service from home. For the first year or so, you should be able to manage perfectly well producing your own letterheads and invoices – especially if you have a good word processor and printer. Printing costs can run very high once you go beyond the business card stage. However, some word-processing services *do* have professionally printed stationery and this has the advantage of looking really businesslike.

You may be able to co-operate with a small local printer. Many of these do not employ a professional WP operator and are often asked to typeset or produce word-processed documents ready for photocopying or printing. You may be in a position to help each other: you by filling the printer's need for an occasional computer typesetter/WP operator, probably at a reduced rate, and the printer by offering you special rates for your own (and your customers') printing needs. My own company currently operates a similar, profitable, reciprocal arrangement with a printer who offers complementary services to our own.

Special offers

The most obvious time to offer a special rate is when you first start up your service. You want to attract customers who will (hopefully) be so impressed by your service that they will be happy to pay the 'normal' rate subsequently. One good way of promoting your service is to offer word-processing at half-price for the first month of business. You could also encourage small businesses to give you a try by offering to do one small 'free' assignment without obligation, followed by a reduced rate for the next month or so.

Marketing is more than simply selling your service

Good promotion of your service does not simply involve putting a few ads in the paper. You must be sure that your word-processing service is suitable for the market at which it is aimed. Is there a need that is not being filled? Can you offer something a little different that will attract custom to you rather than to the established services? Are you in a position to alter your strategy if you find the potential market is not as you anticipated?

A flexible approach is essential. You must be prepared to gear your word-processing service to the market that arises. You might initially direct your service towards overflow work for local businesses with other word-processing as a sideline for example. But if you find that you are actually being asked to prepare quite a lot of résumés, you may need to rethink your original policy and perhaps promote a comprehensive CV service while retaining the overflow work as the sideline. Don't feel you have to stick to your original plan if there is obviously a better market to be had in a slightly different field.

Successful marketing therefore involves researching the word-processing market and your competitors in advance, devising a sensible pricing policy that will allow you a realistic profit margin, adopting a flexible approach (at least for the first year), launching a well-planned advertising campaign and catering for a word-processing need that your competitors have overlooked.

Marketing does not stop once you have acquired a good supply of customers. If you want your service to remain successful, you need to be constantly thinking of ways to improve it, ever watchful of new opportunities and new developments. Remember that *other* word-processing services will also be trying to compete with *you*. Don't allow complacency to turn what could be a very successful service into one that simply ticks over from day to day.

Your personal image

One final point to consider when promoting your business is the image you yourself present. Are you confident and outgoing? Do you quickly put people at ease? Are you able to direct a conversation and ask relevant questions without appearing rude? Can you maintain a professional and mature approach even under pressure, for example when several new clients turn up at once, or when a client disagrees with you?

The public image of your word-processing service will be as much influenced by your own personality and how well you can deal with people as by your qualifications and skills. This is especially true when dealing with customers over the telephone. For home-based word-processing services, this is how initial contact with most potential customers is made. You will have a great variety of customers. Some will have a list of questions ready to ask you and a very good idea of what is involved in their particular assignment. Others won't have the faintest idea where to start. You will need to be able to adapt to either type, providing relevant information quickly and efficiently in the first case and encouraging your contact to divulge his needs and explaining how you can fill them in the second.

Once you are dealing with customers face to face, you will need to maintain the image you initiated over the telephone. Your manner and ability to deal efficiently with the necessities of ascertaining their requirements will be as influential as your ability to produce a high quality piece of work.

The image of your word-processing service will also be enhanced by an attractive office. Your clients will be more impressed if you can interview them in a clean, tidy room where your samples, workstation, pens and paper are all to hand and obviously well organised than they will be if you interview them in an untidy living room with the baby climbing up your legs and the family cat sitting on a dusty word processor in the middle of a cluttered dining table!

Chapter 6
Tools of the Trade

Setting up your office

Although a home-based word-processing service does not make great demands in terms of storage or workspace, you should consider carefully where in your home to set up your office. A spare room is clearly the ideal situation. Here you can have a desk, all your equipment to hand, plenty of storage space and, if the room is large enough, a tidy quiet area in which to receive your customers. Remember though that if you use the room exclusively for your word-processing service and claim it as a tax expense, you could be liable for capital gains tax when you sell your home.

It doesn't matter if you haven't got a separate room from which to operate your word-processing service. Few home-based businesses do in the initial stages. You can start a word-processing service using a walk-in cupboard as your office or even a desk or table in the corner of a room. You could work in your garden shed (provided it is completely dry, weather-proof, warm and secure) or use part of the garage or loft. One ingenious lady converted her understair 'glory hole' into a very neat mini-office: she installed an electric light and socket, shelves for her files, made a fitted desk unit for her word processor and added a telephone extension.

When deciding which part of your home to use you should consider the following factors:

1. Will you be able to leave your equipment set up there, and will it be safe from interference?
2. Will you have enough space to keep several files and books (dictionaries, address books etc) close to hand and safe?
3. Will you be able to work there at any time (when children are playing or in bed; when your partner is watching television) or will you be restricted to certain hours? Remember that business men and students often want word-processing done at short notice, which may involve working during the evening or at weekends.

4. Will you be comfortable working there perhaps for several hours at a time? Cramped conditions, bad seating or lighting and inconvenient access to files and books can be very draining, and will slow you down.

A final consideration when deciding on the location of your office is ease of access to the telephone. Once your business is moving, you will find that you are receiving and making many calls a day. It can be frustrating to have to keep leaving your workstation to trek through to the hall to answer the telephone every 10 minutes. If you cannot reach the telephone without getting up from your desk, you should seriously consider fitting an extension. Since December 1986, it has been legal for anyone to install an extension socket in their own home, but you will need one of the 'modern' master telephone sockets which allow you to unplug your handset. If you have an older style socket, British Telecom will perform a conversion (total cost £28.75 in 1990). You can then purchase and fit a telephone extension kit for about £10 and buy a perfectly good telephone which will plug into it for under £20. An alternative is to purchase a cordless phone to replace your main handset. You can then take the telephone with you wherever you go (up to about 100 m from the base unit). These are still expensive: expect to pay about £70–£80.

Selecting and purchasing 'capital' equipment

Once you have decided where you are going to operate your business, you will have to decide what equipment you need to buy. This section covers your 'non-renewable' or 'capital' equipment needs; that is, equipment that is not actually used up as part of the business (except, of course, for normal wear and tear) such as your desk, word processor, printer, software, stapler, hole-punch, waste bin, calculator and so on. These are items that will appear as the 'assets' of your business in your annual balance sheet. Renewable supplies which are used up as part of your service, such as paper, envelopes, ribbons, staples and so on, are considered on page 111; these will be included as 'expenses' in your profit and loss account.

Furniture and fittings

There is very little point in rushing out and buying a brand new office desk when you first set up your service. These are unnecessarily expensive and often far too large and cumbersome to fit comfortably into a small room. You can use a spare table (preferably one that you can fit drawers or a filing cabinet underneath) but make sure that it is a suitable height for your keyboard. Most dining tables are too high to work at comfortably. If you are trying to keep costs down, you can actually make a perfectly adequate desk by resting a smooth door on breezeblocks, a pair of old bedside cabinets or a pair of two-drawer filing cabinets.

If you decide to invest in a desk, consider a second-hand office or teacher's desk, or one of the do-it-yourself variety that comes in kit form. A second-hand office desk that is in good condition is probably the best buy as it will be strong and durable and of better quality than a 'kit' desk. You should also be able to sell it later on for much the same price as you pay for it, provided you keep it in good condition. Many office suppliers sell second-hand desks. Alternatively, look in the classified ads under 'Office Equipment'. You should find a number of firms selling off old office furniture. Another good source of quality second-hand desks is auction sales – either purely office furniture auctions or general auction sales. Most large towns have a sale-room with auctions once or twice a week; these will be advertised in the local press.

When you go out in search of your desk, take a tape-measure with you and the measurements of your room. You need to be sure that you can accommodate it. Decide beforehand whether you want a single pedestal desk, one with drawers at both sides, one with a built-in filing cabinet at one side and drawers at the other, or whatever. Check that the drawers slide in and out easily and that the desk stands solidly without rocking when pushed. Run your hand across the top. Is the surface smooth or does it have grooves or splinters that will make writing difficult? Is the top large enough to be used both as a word processor stand and as a writing surface or would you be better off with a small writing desk and a separate word processor/computer workstation? These latter units are very popular nowadays and can often save space (usually the printer, if separate, is stored below or behind the word processor), but many are grossly over-priced and you will need to measure up carefully to be sure that your equipment will fit comfortably in the spaces allocated.

What about a filing cabinet? Although these are useful, they do tend to be rather expensive, especially new. If you can get an office desk with a built-in single-drawer filing cabinet at one side, this will probably suffice. Alternatively, you can get a two-drawer 'kit' filing cabinet for about £60 new, or a steel four-drawer filing cabinet for about £80. Again, buying a second-hand cabinet is probably the answer. Unfortunately, second-hand filing cabinets are rarely in such good condition as second-hand desks. Small dents in the front and sides don't really matter so long as they don't interfere with the sliding drawer mechanism or the lock, and you can brighten up a chipped grey filing cabinet with bright paint. Make sure that the drawers slide in and out easily and that the file hanging runners (inside the drawers) are intact and not rusting or bent.

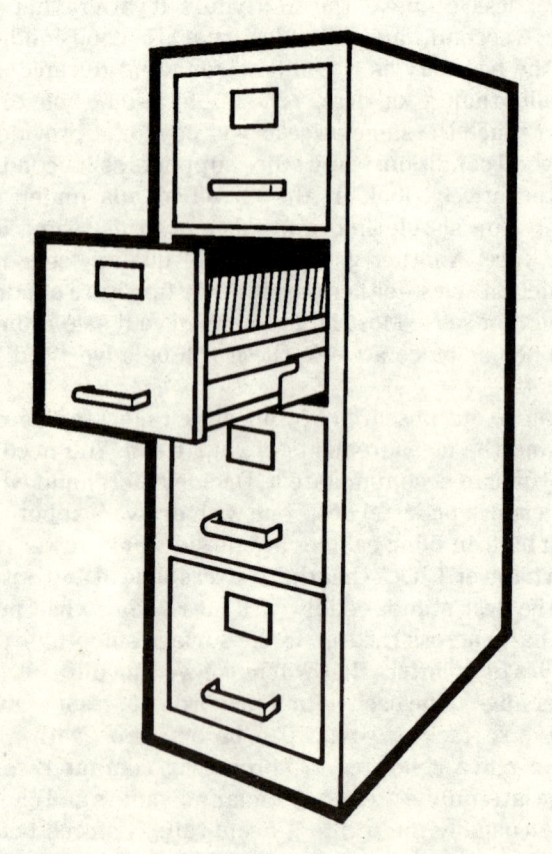

Four-drawer filing cabinet

You will also need shelf space on which to store books, directories and manuals. If you don't already have shelving, you can construct cheap shelves yourself using planks of wood supported by bricks, or buy shelf-making kits. The ideal place for shelves is over or next to your workstation so that you can reach your files and books without having to leave your seat.

A comfortable chair is another essential. Don't skimp on this or you will pay for it with backache and a stiff neck. It is well worth investing in a proper typist's chair. This should have an adjustable back rest, adjustable height and preferably a swivel base and wheels. It *is* possible to buy second-hand chairs but test them out carefully as most second-hand office chairs really are on their last legs! With the advent of home computing, many modern furniture retailers are now selling 'computer chairs' at a fraction of the cost of a new 'office' model. These are not quite so well made but can be substantially cheaper. Go for one with a cloth rather than a vinyl seat. Vinyl is prone to splitting and can become rather uncomfortable in hot weather! Expect to pay around £50–£120 (or more) for a good, new, office model and upwards of £20 for a 'look-alike' home-computing chair.

Lighting is also important. If you haven't got a good overhead light above your desk, then you will need to invest in an anglepoise reading lamp. These are not expensive, but make sure that you can use at least a 60 W bulb in the lamp and that you will have adequate space to erect it so that it shines on to your work from the side or behind you. Don't make do with a table lamp or work in a dim corner of the room. You will be slowed down by eyestrain and lack of concentration if you cannot see the copy clearly.

Typewriters
This book is primarily intended for people interested in setting up and running a word-processing service; therefore, only brief mention is made here of typewriters.

Electric and electronic typewriters are still popular in business, but if you abhor the thought of word-processing or cannot afford WP equipment, you *can* run a typing service using one of these. They have fallen in price in recent years in line with the fall in the price of WPs and a new portable model can now be acquired for about £150. A more advanced model will cost more but is well worth the investment. The Sharp PA-3140, for example, is almost a word processor. It has a one-line correction memory, two-line display, 15 kb memory, spell correction and thesaurus facilities, search and replace, justification and more, and retails for about £250.

As with your other equipment, shop around for the most

suitable model for your needs and try to arrange for back-up and maintenance in the event of breakdown.

Word processors

What does a word processor do?
This section serves as a basic introduction for the unitiated. Skip it if you are already familiar with the capabilities of a word processor.

A word processor is like a typewriter with expanded capabilities. You can use it to write anything you wish in the same way you'd use a typewriter. But unlike a typewriter, a word processor will let you edit or reformat your document easily, without retyping. A word processor uses a keyboard like a typewriter. As you type on to the keyboard, the text you are typing will appear on a screen. You don't have to print your document on to paper until you're ready. This allows you to modify your text over and over again on the screen before printing.

With a word processor, there's no need to press the <ENTER> key (like the RETURN key on a typewriter) after typing each line of text. All word processors have automatic 'wordwrapping': your text will automatically wrap around to the next line when it reaches the right margin. This feature will speed up your typing considerably.

A computer word processor comprises 'hardware' (a computer, visual display unit, disk drive and printer) and 'software' (the program which instructs the computer to operate as a word processor). The basic components are:

- A standard qwerty keyboard which will also have special 'function' and 'control' keys.
- A visual display unit (a screen on which you can see the text prior to printing) sometimes called a monitor or VDU for short.
- A central processing unit (CPU) which enables the equipment to carry out automatic functions such as editing, storage and retrieval.
- A printer on which the finished product will be produced.
- Some sort of storage/retrieval mechanism (usually a disk drive) which allows you to 'store' text for future use. The word-processing program itself will probably also be stored on disks.

Most word processors are supplied with an instruction pack-

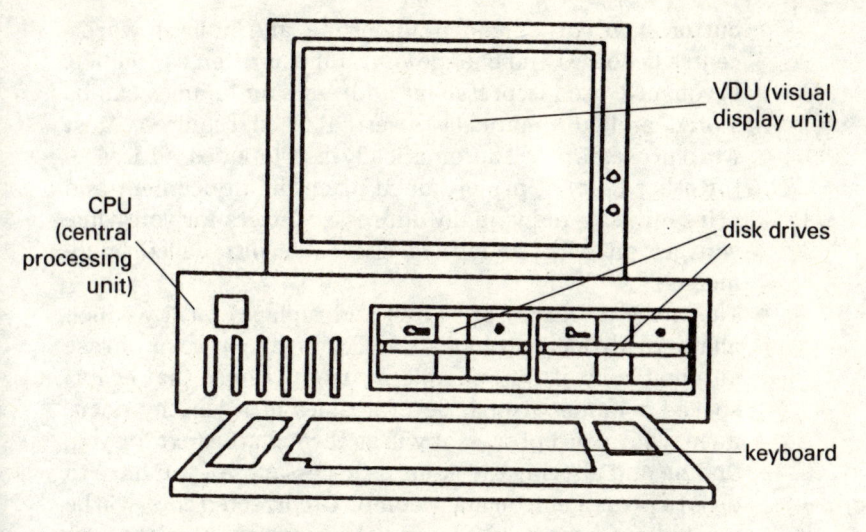

The basic components of a word processor

age which teaches you how to use your particular model. If you've never used (or even seen) a word processor before don't be put off by its apparent complexity. With a little time and patience, you will find that it is really very easy to operate and a great improvement on both electric and electronic typewriters. If you are still doubtful, enrol on a short word-processing course to get the feel of using one before you decide whether or not to buy.

There are many different word-processing programs available currently. A brief review of some current packages is given later in this chapter. They vary slightly in the functions they can perform or, more often, in the *way* they perform those functions. So what do word processors actually do?

- They allow you to see, alter and correct text as you type it and before it is finally printed. You can quickly insert, delete, copy or move any amount of text quickly and easily. You can also do this with documents that you have keyed in previously and 'stored'.
- They can (if you wish) automatically produce straight right and left margins to your work (called justification).
- They can 'store' text so that if your customer comes back with revisions, these can be made quickly and easily and without retyping the whole document.
- Most can produce subscripts, superscripts, symbols, 'headers' and 'footers', and various typefaces at the push of a

button. You can enbolden, underline, and italicise words, centre headings and change your mind as often as you like.
- Frequently used expressions, addresses and names can be stored and automatically inserted when required. Most word processors will automatically insert names/addresses (or other text) at pre-ordained places in a document and print out, say, individually addressed letters for you while you get on with something else (a facility called 'mail-merge').
- They have a search (or search and replace) facility which allows you to locate (or locate and change) a word or phrase automatically. If, for example, a customer finds that he has spelled a name wrongly several times in a lengthy document, your word processor will go through the text for you, finding and altering the name as necessary. All you have to do is to press a button and a complete corrected copy will be printed automatically. You can also move about in the text very quickly any time you like.
- They can automatically number pages, count words and tabulate. Many allow you to produce text in columns (like a newspaper), import graphics or 'draw' on the screen, input text in a variety of founts and view the document exactly as it will appear when printed out (a facility called 'WYSIWYG' – meaning 'what you see is what you get').
- Dictionary programs are available (or built into the word-processing program) which will go through the text checking and correcting spelling mistakes (and many typographical errors) in your script. These can save time during proof-reading and can usually be amended to include any unusual words or names that you use frequently. Some of the more advanced programs even have a grammar-checking facility!

Computers
One of the first decisions you must make is the choice of 'hardware' – the physical components of your system. You can buy a dedicated word processor (ie one that can't be used for anything other than word-processing) or a ready-made word-processing (WP) package (a computer, printer and word processing program), or opt for purchasing the various components separately.

Dedicated word processors
Dedicated word processors often have the keyboard, screen (or VDU), disk drive (if any) and printing component all housed in

one compact unit. The Brother EM-1050 (retailing at under £500) and the Smith Corona PWP 1000 (under £250) are such word processors. The Smith Corona PWP 7000 (under £500) is a compact, portable model with a separate daisy-wheel printer. These are all perfectly good word processors (although the Smith Corona PWP 7000 keyboard is rather cramped for my liking) with all the usual word-processing features. However, there is little benefit in limiting yourself solely to word-processing by buying a 'dedicated' machine. It limits the range of business services you can offer and may be more difficult to resell than a PC.

Ready-made WP packages

One alternative is to opt for a ready-made WP package. The most popular are those in the Amstrad range. The Amstrad PCW8256 comes complete with its own word-processing program called LocoScript and a 9-pin dot-matrix printer. By shopping around, you should be able to get one for under £350. Upgraded versions which have twice as much memory are the PCW8512 and PCW9512 which currently retail at under £500 (including a daisy-wheel printer). LocoScript is a reasonable word-processing program which is well liked by those who use it but the printer supplied with the PCW8256 package produces rather poor quality print and is not likely to be robust enough for a hard-working word-processing service. Shop around for a good price. You may find that you can get a much better deal if you order by post (the monthly magazine *Computer Shopper* is good for this). The Amstrad PCW9512 with word-processing software, a daisy-wheel printer, cut-sheet feeder and one year on-site maintenance was recently offered at only £399 (plus VAT and carriage) for example. A limited range of business software can now be acquired for these semi-dedicated machines.

Purchasing separate components

If you opt for purchasing the various components of your word-processing system separately, you will be spoilt for choice. The recent boom in micro-computers and personal computers (PCs) means that there is now a very wide range on offer. Unless you want to start off with the bare minimum and work up, you will need at least a 'PC'. This merely means a computer which is compatible with the industry standard IBM PC. (You may also come across the terms 'XT' and 'AT' which were also generated originally by IBM to refer to their higher standard models.)

'Home' computers, intended for personal use and games, rarely have sufficient memory to run more than the most basic word-processing programs and will usually be rather slow and unable to hold much more than 10-15 pages of text (necessitating lots of saving/retrieving). Having said that, I do know of one successful word-processing service which started up with nothing more than an Amstrad 664 (the now obsolete disk version of the ever popular 464), a copy of Tasword 664 and a cheap, 9-pin, Epson printer!

PCs continue to fall in price and most manufacturers currently produce a model that will be perfectly satisfactory for a home-based word-processing service for under £500. Examples include the Amstrad PC1512, PC1640 and PC2086 (which have increasing memory respectively and prices starting at under £350 for the PC1512), the Commodore PC10SD starter pack (which includes training video, typing tutor, word-processing software, database and spreadsheet facilities), the Olivetti PCS86 and the Opus PCIIISF. All of these PCs include a keyboard, CPU, disk drive and monochrome VDU. You should also be able to get 12 months free on-site maintenance with any of the above. You would pay somewhat more for a colour VDU (slightly better for some word-processing programs but you can manage without) and an extra built-in disk drive. (Alternatively, you can buy an add-on separate disk drive for about £80.) A second disk drive can be very useful with certain word-processing programs which require you to leave the program disk in the drive while you are using it. With a second disk drive, you can store and retrieve text from a 'storage' disk without having to remove and replace the program disk several times.

On the matter of disk drives and disks, you should note that there are currently two sizes of 'industry standard' floppy disk. These are either $3\frac{1}{2}''$ disks housed in a hard plastic casing or $5\frac{1}{4}''$ disks housed in a softer card (or plastic) casing. Most good software now comes in both formats. However, the biggest computer company in the world (IBM) has standardised on the more robust and higher capacity $3\frac{1}{2}''$ disk and, as a result, everyone else is doing the same. To this end, $5\frac{1}{4}''$ disks and drives are likely to be phased out over the next decade. The Amstrad PCWs (and their home computer CPCs) use a unique, non-standard, disk ($3\frac{1}{4}''$) and drive which might restrict the type of software you can use. As well as buying your software programs on disk, you will need a good supply of 'blank' disks on which to store text. You can store an enormous amount of information on a disk (25,000 words on a $5\frac{1}{4}''$) and they can be 'read' extremely quickly.

3½" floppy disk *5¼" floppy disk*

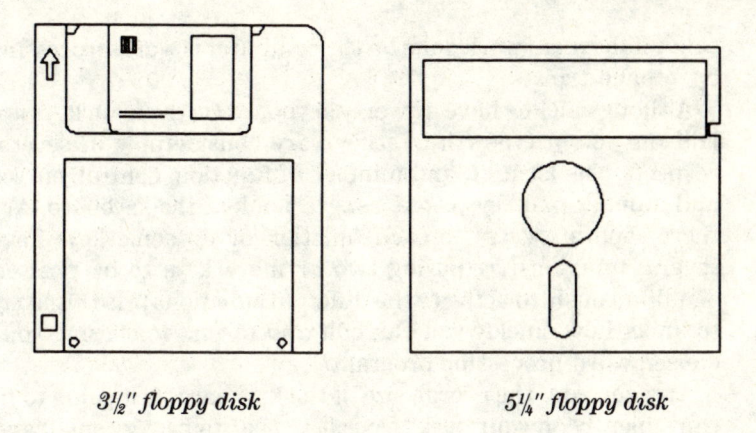

If you are prepared to pay a little more for your PC (upwards of £700), you should be able to get a model which has both a 'floppy' disk drive and a 'hard' disk drive. The hard disk is permanently housed inside the CPU and is accessed through the keyboard. It has an enormous capacity - 160,000 words or more on a relatively small 1 Mb hard disk - and will hold your word-processing program (as well as several other programs) together with all the text you will need store. You will probably want to keep 'back-up' copies of certain documents, as well as your word-processing program, on floppy disks in case your hard disk fails or your computer breaks down.

All of the leading manufacturers produce hard-disk PCs with variable amounts of 'memory' (measured in megabytes or Mb) and choice of colour or mono VDU. Amstrad has a 30 Mb hard-disk PC1640 (mono monitor) at the bottom of its range, which retails for about £700. At the top of its range is the PC2386, which has a 65 Mb hard disk and will cost you about £1000 more. Commodore's 20 Mb PC20III retails for about £700 plus VAT, as does the Opus PCIII (20 Mb). It is unlikely that you will need more than 20-30 Mb of memory while you are running your word-processing business single-handed (unless you are planning to use a lot of other business programs as well), so don't splash out on something too expensive to start with!

Since most of the leading makes of computer are reliable, likely to be offered with on-site maintenance and have very similar facilities for roughly the same price, you will need to consider other factors when deciding which one to buy. The major one (in my opinion) is the keyboard. This seems to have little relevance to the enthusiastic computer user but is of considerable importance if the main work done on the computer is word-processing by a touch-typist.

Although all PCs have a qwerty keyboard (ie the main keys are laid out like a typewriter), they vary considerably in several respects. The location and number of function, control, cursor and number-pad keys is one aspect. Look at the keyboard. Are there separate keys for each function or do some keys have several functions (requiring two or more keys to be pressed simultaneously to activate the different functions)? Is this likely to affect how quickly you can edit and format text using your chosen word-processing program?

Also consider the overall size of the keyboard. Is it going to fit conveniently on your desk? Does it appear to be very small and cramped? Is the keyboard set at an angle that will make typing comfortable? Are the 'shift' keys, the RETURN/ENTER key, the backspace/delete key and the 'tab' key easy to reach and of a good size?

Where are the <ctrl> and <alt> keys located? On many keyboards these are very close to (often underneath) the shift keys. This can cause problems for a touch-typist since the <ctrl> and <alt> keys, when pressed in conjunction with another key, usually have a formatting or editing effect; for example <alt> and <c> when pressed together often have the effect of centring the current typing line or paragraph. This can be a bit frustrating if you expected to see a capital 'C' on the screen! However, this kind of problem does tend to rectify itself once you get used to your particular keyboard and your fingers 'learn' how far to move to press a particular key.

The actual 'feel' of the keys as you press them is probably more significant. Try typing on the keyboard for a while. The keys should move a sufficient distance for you to be sure that you have engaged them and should provide some audible indication that they have been pressed (a click). Virtually all computer keys have a repeating function. This will not need extra *pressure* to engage (unlike a typewriter key) but should require the key to remain depressed for slightly longer than a single stroke. Check that this is the case.

Also consider the size of the keys relative to your fingers, the feel of the top of the keys (is there a depression which helps to guide your fingers towards the centre?) and the spacing (are they so close together that your hands feel cramped?). Is the space bar a convenient size and located correctly for typing? Is there a sloping area below the space bar where you can rest your lower palms during pauses, without removing your fingers from the 'home keys' and without pressing on the space bar or other keys?

Although most computers now come as a 'package', it is possible to buy keyboards separately if you are really fussy. They cost anywhere from £50 to £100. If you do this, you will need to ensure that your chosen keyboard and CPU are compatible.

You should also ask about on-site maintenance. Most PCs now come with 12 months free on-site maintenance and you should certainly ask for this if it isn't automatically offered by your supplier. Also ask about the cost of continuing the maintenance agreement beyond the first year. On-site maintenance is essential (unless you have a back-up machine) since sending your equipment away for repair can take weeks. Ask about the details of the maintenance agreement. How quickly will the engineer come after your call? Does the agreement cover replacement of parts and does the supplier stock these? Would an alternative machine be made available to you if yours had to be sent away for repair or if parts had to be ordered?

Printers

There are two types of printer: *impact* (in which the print head strikes a carbon ribbon) and *non-impact* (in which there is no contact with the paper). For economical reasons, impact printers are currently the most popular among individuals and small businesses.

Impact printers

There are basically two types of impact printer: dot matrix and daisy wheel.

Dot-matrix printers form letters using tiny dots made by a matrix of 'pins' the size of one print position. When a character is to be printed, the appropriate pattern of pins is activated to form the character and this strikes the ribbon. The quality of the finished product is influenced by the number of dots used to form each letter. This in turn depends on the number of pins in the print head and how many times the print head passes over the same printing line (slightly offset on a return passage to fill in the spaces).

Dot-matrix printers are very versatile and can produce graphics (charts and diagrams) as well as a wide variety of text styles. They are also relatively cheap. If you decide on one of these, make sure that you purchase one that has a facility for producing 'near-letter quality' (NLQ) print. On a good printer, this should be almost indistinguishable from true 'type-print' because the dots are so close together.

The accepted standard for an NLQ printer is one with at least an 18-pin print head – a 24-pin print head would be better. Some 9-pin printers claim to produce NLQ (eg the Star LC-10 MkII) and can be purchased for about £150, but the quality is not likely to be good enough for most of your customers. You will pay at least £200 for a basic 24-pin model intended for personal/study work. If you want a more substantial, heavy duty, model, you will pay about £100 more. The Star LC24-10 Panasonic KXP1124 and Oki ML-380 are suitable starter printers for a home-based word-processing service and all currently retail for under £300.

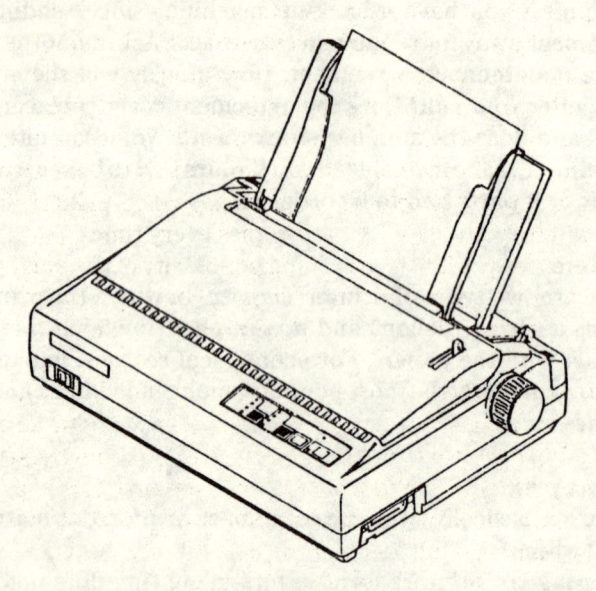

Dot-matrix printer

Daisy-wheel (or 'letter quality') printers generally cost slightly more and print more slowly. However, the quality of print is usually superior to that of NLQ dot-matrix printers. The printing element, as the name suggests, is arranged like the petals of a daisy. The petals consist of flexible arms radiating from a central spindle. At the end of each arm is a typehead. The printing element rotates at high speed to bring each typehead into the correct position for printing. The wheel can easily be changed so that different typefaces can be used (but you will need to purchase a variety of daisy wheels to do this). The main disadvantages of daisy wheels are that there is no facility for producing graphics and they have a rather restricted character set. Theoretically, you could change wheels to produce italics or other special characters, but this is very tedious and time consuming. A good, durable, daisy-wheel printer will probably cost you between £300 and £500. Extra wheels will cost more.

Daisy-wheel (and the related golf-ball and thimble) printers are now becoming relatively rare. This is partially because of the restricted character set, the fact that economical models are slow and that they cannot produce graphics. It is also because the NLQ print of a good 24-pin (or more) dot-matrix printer has improved so much in recent years that it is almost impossible to distinguish from true type-print. Dot-matrix printers also have the advantage that you can produce 'draft' copies quickly and cheaply. This is often an asset to a word-processing service since you can provide an initial draft relatively quickly (and cheaply since less ink is used and the wear on your printer is reduced) and then run off the finished NLQ version when your customer has agreed the final revisions. With a daisy-wheel printer, you are restricted to running off quality copies every time.

Another reason for the declining popularity of the daisy-wheel printer is the recent fall in price of the vastly superior non-impact printers.

Non-impact printers

Non-impact printers are of two main types: ink jet and laser.

The ink-jet printer squirts ink at the paper through a series of nozzles as the print head passes over the paper. Laser printers operate in a similar way to photocopiers. These printers are quiet, fast and produce a superior print quality. Because there is no fixed print head, they can produce excellent graphics and a vast range of point sizes, typefaces and styles. If you can stretch to one of these, it will produce print of an excellent quality which will be a great asset to your business. By shopping around, you should be able to get a good quality ink-jet printer (eg the Canon BubbleJet or the HP QuietJet) for under £500. Laser printers (currently the 'cream' of the printer world) cost more but are still falling in price. The original 'industry standard' HP LaserJet IIP (or one of its many clones) can now be acquired for under £900 and is an excellent machine for a word-processing service if you can afford one! Other laser printers selling at about the same price are the Epson GQ5000, the Oki 400 and the Sanyo SPX-608. The more expensive models have additional facilities, eg automatic double-sided printing, very fast printing times or colour printing.

Another advantage of laser and most ink-jet printers is that they come equipped with at least one paper feed tray. This can save considerable time in 'hand feeding' paper into the printer. You can get 'cut-sheet feeders' for most good impact printers but these will cost you anything from £60 to £200 on top of the price of the printer. Most dot-matrix and some daisy-wheel printers will also take continuous stationery – the kind with holes down the side which feeds into the printer using a tractor-feed system – and this can cut costs for drafts and for your own letters and invoices.

The pros and cons
Again, the type of printer you choose will depend on the kind of service you intend to offer as well as the constraints of your purse. If you are going to be providing secretarial services for small businesses, you will probably opt for an impact printer (which can produce carbon copies) – you may be happy with a daisy-wheel printer since you probably won't need a range of point sizes or typefaces. A good quality dot-matrix printer with NLQ will be the ideal choice if your service is going to be more varied but you wish to keep costs down. Finally, an ink-jet or laser printer will be your choice if you are prepared to invest more in your business at the outset (or expect it to expand rapidly), if you want to branch into related areas (eg desktop publishing) and if you wish to make full use of the features provided by your word-processing program.

One other thing you will need to consider when you purchase your printer is how you are going to connect it to your computer and whether the machines will 'understand' one another. You want to be sure that what appears on your screen is what you end up with printed on a sheet of paper! To this end, computer and printer manufacturers have agreed on standard junctions (interfaces) between computer and printer and a fairly standard code of electronic messages sent between them. The usual junction is either a 'Centronics' (parallel) interface or an 'RS-232' (serial) interface. Your computer/printer manuals will tell you which type of interface (connecting cable) to buy. If in doubt, ask your supplier.

The most common code used to store information in a word processor and to transfer it to a printer is ASCII (American Standard Code for Information Interchange), an example of which is shown in the table on page 95. You can see from the table that 'A' is 65 and 'a' is 97. The word 'Cat' when typed in on the keyboard will appear in the computer's memory and be 'sent' to the printer as 67 97 116. The values from 0 to 32 and 127 onwards are control characters which are not printable. For example, code 13 is carriage return; when you press the <ENTER> or RETURN key, this code is stored in the text and subsequently sent to the printer. The main problem with this code system is that there are slight variations between manufacturers. As you can see from the table, code 96 *usually* specifies a 'pound sign'. You will find that, with some word processors, the '£' key on the keyboard does not correspond to a pound sign on the screen and/or in print. This is the most common problem and can be

Code	Meaning	Code	Meaning	Code	Meaning
32	Space	61	=	90	Z
33	!	62	>	91	[
34	"	63	?	92	\
35	#	64	@	93	]
36	§	65	A	94	^
37	%	66	B	95	_
38	&	67	C	96	£
39	'	68	D	97	a
40	(	69	E	98	b
41	)	70	F	99	c
42	*	71	G	100	d
43	+	72	H	101	e
44	@	73	I	102	f
45	-	74	J	103	g
46	.	75	K	104	h
47	/	76	L	105	i
48	0	77	M	106	j
49	1	78	N	107	k
50	2	79	O	108	l
51	3	80	P	109	m
52	4	81	Q	110	n
53	5	82	R	111	o
54	6	83	S	112	p
55	7	84	T	113	q
56	8	85	U	114	r
57	9	86	V	115	s
58	:	87	W	116	t
59	;	88	X	117	u
60	<	89	Y	118	v

ASCII character codes

annoying, although it is usually fairly easy to rectify. Your word-processing program will normally ask you to specify the kind of computer and printer you are using as part of the initial configuration and this usually prevents interface problems. If in doubt, you should ask your dealer whether the computer, program and printer you have chosen are compatible.

When considering the type, make and price of printer you intend to buy, you should also consider the cost of replaceable items such as alternative daisy wheels, ribbons, and ink and toner cartridges. Carbon ribbons for impact printers cost anything from £2 to £5 each (depending on the manufacturer and the number you buy). Buying them in bulk by post from one of the big suppliers will work out a lot cheaper than buying a few at a time from a local supplier. It may be worth giving preference to the printer manufacturer's own ribbons. Cheap 'clones' are available for most makes of printer. (I know of people who swear by them, but I have generally found them to be unreliable – the ribbon being too wet initially causing smearing and then, perversely, drying out too quickly.)

You also need to get an on-site maintenance contract for your printer (this should be free for at least the first year). Enquire at the same time about the availability of replacement parts (eg new print heads), how fast service is likely to be and whether you will be able to have a replacement printer immediately should yours have to be sent away for repair.

Hardware accessories

Following swiftly in the footsteps of the computer boom came the computer accessory boom. None of the items mentioned here are in any way essential to the running of your service or to the safety or operation of your equipment. They are mentioned merely because they exist and may be useful! Don't buy them straight away – see if you need them first.

One problem that some people experience when they have to watch a VDU for a long period of time is eye-strain. If you have this problem, and it is not alleviated by adjusting the brightness and contrast on your screen, you can fit an anti-glare screen to your monitor for about £20.

If you want to keep your equipment clean and protected when not in use, you can purchase relatively cheap dust covers for your printer, VDU and keyboard. You can also buy a type-through plastic cover for your keyboard if you want to protect it from dust, dirt and coffee spills!

An impact printer can create a lot of noise in a small room. A rubber mat will help to alleviate this. You can also get enclosing noise shields but these are rather expensive.

There is a range of accessories designed to make optimum use of space and these may be beneficial if you have very little room. They include 'drawers' for storing your keyboard beneath the VDU/CPU when not in use, swivel stands and arms to move the VDU about on the desk, and printer stands. Other peripherals and accessories such as mice, scanners, extra disk drives, modems, paper feeders and so on are considered elsewhere.

Word-processing programs

You may have acquired a word-processing (WP) program as part of a package deal when you purchased your equipment. If not, you can get a perfectly good basic WP program for your PC for as little as £50 (less for a program for a micro-computer). If you want one of the more advanced, industry standard, programs, you could pay up to 10 times this amount. Your choice will depend on the amount you want to spend, the needs of your word-processing service and possibly the kind of program you are already familiar with.

All of the WP programs reviewed or mentioned here provide the basic features considered earlier. Since WP programs are continuously being produced and updated, much of the information contained here will very soon be out of date. You will need to undertake your own research into what is available currently in order to get the most suitable and economical program for your needs. What follows is a brief review of some programs from the lower, middle and upper price brackets to give you a 'feel' for what's on offer.

LocoScript PC is a popular program in the middle price bracket. It started life as a give-away with Amstrad's PCW but can now be purchased for any PC. It has an add-on database and mail-merge program, an 80,000 word spell-checker (which can be added to), and can provide Greek and Cyrillic characters, accents and chemical symbols in addition to some special print effects such as shadow and outline. It also allows you to display formatting codes within the text if you so wish. This is a useful feature which not all WP programs provide. Unfortunately, you can't change the codes (eg change all underlining to italics), or line spacing, as a formatting mechanism (ie you have to work through the text changing the codes as you go). Another drawback is that you can't work on two documents simultaneously and there is no help system. Also, the pull-down menus are supposed to be self-explanatory – but aren't! Having said that, this program has received very good reviews recently (which is why it is included here) and you might like it more than I did!

LocoScript PC is probably very good for people upgrading from a PCW to a PC who are already familiar with it – and it is certainly well liked by PCW users. It currently retails at between £90 and £125 (shop around) or less for the PCW version upgrade. Contact Locomotive Software (0306 740606) for more information.

Two slightly more expensive programs which have been launched recently are Multiwriter (Data Liberation Limited – 0983 864674) and Top Copy Professional (Top Level Computing Limited – 0453 753955), both of which retail for around £200.

If your word-processing service is extensively geared to foreign languages, Multiwriter is well worth considering. It allows you to print in English, Albanian, Dutch, French and other European languages as well as some obscurities such as Hebrew, Macedonian and Esperanto. You can write on screen in two different tongues and have both character sets operational simultaneously. The program also includes a spell-checker.

Top Copy Professional is a reasonable WP program which allows you to produce text in newspaper columns if desired and in a range of founts. It has all the usual advanced features such as multiple document working, spell-checker and mail-merge, and is supplied with a self-teaching tutorial package and three months free telephone support.

At the top end of the range are the well-known packages such as: Multimate (a Wang-like processor) which includes a grammar-checker in its most recent version (Multimate 4.0) and can be purchased for under £350; WordPerfect (currently version 5.1) which has an unrivalled depth of functionality and retails for under £300; and Wordstar (V6.0), once the industry standard, which retails for under £250. All of these are fast, efficient, powerful programs which should more than suffice for the needs of any word-processing service. However, they are *very* expensive and it is doubtful whether you will need all of the features offered by such programs while you are working on your own from home. On the other hand, it is more likely that you are already familiar with one of these programs.

These programs are popular with big businesses and courses which aim to give you a good grounding in Multimate, WordPerfect or Wordstar are held regularly all over the country. Unfortunately, such courses are rather expensive – you are likely to pay £150–£350 for the privilege of learning how to use the package! On the positive side, most suppliers will be able to give you a demonstration disk for any of the above programs which will at least let you see what you would be buying and whether it would be suitable for your needs. Unless you are really keen on one of these programs, buy something cheaper to start with. (Dedicated WordPerfect fans can get a copy of Personal WordPerfect for under £130. This cut-down version offers a thesaurus, outliner and so on but no mail-merge facility.)

Finally, this brings us to the cheaper WP programs available currently such as Tasword PC (retailing at under £50), Top Copy Plus (retailing at under £70) and First Word+ (retailing at under £60). These programs are all perfectly adequate for a home-based word-processing service and will offer all the facilities you will need initially. Once your service is operational, you will be able to judge what extra or alternative word-processing facilities will be of most use to you. That will be the time to consider purchasing a different, more expensive, package.

Tasword PC (Tasman Software Limited - 0532 438301) is a good basic program with a relatively concise, easy to understand, instruction manual and a built-in tutorial program. It started life as a 'home computer' WP program which has been upgraded for use on PCs. It has all the usual WP features including the use of marker commands which allow you to move automatically to pre-selected locations within the text (useful for forms or standard invoices), search and replace, headers/footers, an alternative character set, a 'notepad' system, user-definable keys (useful for saving/retrieving frequently used phrases) word/line count and page numbering. The program also allows you to change the ASCII codes in the program - this is a bonus as you can configure the keyboard to suit your own needs (eg to produce characters with accents).

One major drawback of this program is that there is no built-in spell-checker. You can buy one separately (TasSpell PC) but you will have to pay about £40 for the privilege and it is abysmally slow. In addition, you can't hold two text files in memory simultaneously - a facility which I find essential but some word-processing services seem to manage without. You can get a demonstration disk from Tasman Software to try out the program before committing yourself to buying the full version.

Another WP program I quite like is BetterWorking Word Publisher (Spinnaker Software, 1 Kendall Square, Cambridge, MA 02139, USA). This is an American program, retailing for under £80 in the UK, which has quasi-desktop publishing features (see Chapter 8). For its price, it is an excellent program with a truly 'user friendly' manual. As well as all the usual WP features (eg mail-merge, word count etc), it allows you to load two documents in memory simultaneously; offers multiple typefaces, a range of user-definable point sizes and different typestyles (bold, italic, underlining, subscript, superscript etc); has the ability to print in newspaper columns (useful for newsletters and leaflets); and can import graphics (pictures) into the text and add horizontal lines and boxes. It also has a built-in and very fast 100,000 word spell-checker, a simple thesaurus and a WYSIWYG viewing option. In addition, it offers an 'outliner' (similar to a notepad) which is really intended for people sketching out the basics of a long report or manuscript and is not likely to be of much use to a word-processing service.

The main drawbacks with Word Publisher relate to the fact that it is American. For example, there is no 'pound' sign on my version (although the manufacturers now claim that they have solved this problem for the British market) and all measurements are in inches (or parts thereof). You will, of course, need a suitable printer (eg an ink-jet, laser or good dot-matrix printer) to take advantage of the facilities offered by this type of program.

As you can see, WP programs do vary. You will need to consider carefully the needs of your word-processing service when deciding which features you require. Once you have a list of the essential features, and have decided how much you are prepared to spend, do some research into the kind of WP programs available. Most dealers will be quite happy either to demonstrate a program or let you experiment with it yourself. In addition, *Computer Shopper*, *Which? Computer*, *Micro Decision*, *What Personal Computer* and *PC User* (among others) regularly review new WP packages. These magazines are also useful sources of information about computers, word processors and printers, and are full of advertisements offering bargain deals and packages.

The first thing you must do when you get your new WP program is to make a copy of it. Floppy disks (especially the 5¼" disks) are easily damaged by heat, cold, moisture, magnetism, coffee spillages, bending and so on. You do not want to risk losing your program. So make a back-up copy – your computer or WP program manual will tell you how to do this – and use the back-up disk(s) for your day-to-day word-processing. Store the original disks somewhere safe. Even if you are installing your program on a relatively protected hard disk, you should take care to store your original disks safely. Hard disks are not immune to problems of their own and you do not want to be in a situation where you are unable to work because your hard disk or computer has failed for some reason. This is also a good reason for backing up all text stored on your hard disk on to floppy disks. Do this regularly – once a week is not too often – to avoid losing assignments should your equipment fail.

Copiers
Whoever you are word-processing for, they will almost certainly want at least one copy of the work. Making carbon copies (or using multi-forms) is a quick and cheap option if you have an impact printer. However, the quality of carbon copies will not be as good as the top copy, you will be limited in the number of copies you can make at one go and you will have to manually feed the paper 'sandwiches' into the printer. If your client wants good quality copies, you will have to run off extra copies on your printer. This can be very time-consuming. It also prevents you from using the printer for anything else and, depending on your WP program, it may also prevent you from doing any word-processing until the print run has finished. The alternative – getting photocopies from a copy-shop – is expensive, time-consuming and inconvenient.

You will probably be happy enough running off additional copies on your printer to start with or occasionally having a bulk run done at your local copy-shop. However, if you find that this is becoming overly time-consuming and costly, you may want to consider buying, or leasing, a photocopier of your own. With your own machine, photocopies will be quick and easy to produce, look better than carbon copies and will allow you some leeway to 'cut and paste' originals (eg to insert tables, pictures etc).

In addition, photocopies sometimes work out cheaper than printed copy. This depends on the type of printer you have and the type of copier you wish to purchase. You will need to undertake a costing exercise to ascertain whether a photocopier will actually produce cheaper 'copies' than you can get already. Take into account the cost of wear and tear on the printer and the ribbon, and the cost of your time in either feeding the printer or losing access to the word processor. Compare this with the cost of using your own photocopier. This will depend on the monthly lease (or purchase price) and maintenance fee, the cost of toner (if this is not included in the maintenance agreement) and the cost of your time. Reduce the figures to a cost per copy for comparison.

This kind of exercise can generate surprising results. When I leased my first free-standing copier, for example, I found the cost of a photocopy to be significantly cheaper than the cost of printing a page using either of my dot-matrix printers but more expensive than the cost of printing a page using my laser printer!

There are other advantages in having your own photocopier. Being able to take a copy of the original (or only) copy of a manuscript can be useful as a precaution against loss or damage. In addition, if your customer has a copy of the assignment, it makes it easier for you to telephone him with any questions, since you can refer to specific pages and line numbers. A photocopier will also be of use in your own work. You can produce your own stationery, advertisements and leaflets. And you may also be able to enhance your service by offering photocopying as an extra facility.

To determine whether the purchase (or lease) of a copier would be feasible for your word-processing service, you should consider the following:

- How many photocopies you currently get per month from a copy-shop.
- What these copies cost.
- How much time you spend travelling to/from and at the copy-shop.
- How much it costs you to get to/from the copy-shop.
- Whether you will advertise photocopying as an extra service.
- Whether a copier would simply pay for itself (ultimately) or whether you would want it to make a profit in its own right.
- What kind of copier would best suit your needs.
- What your copier will cost to buy (or lease) and run.

The cost, size and variety of photocopiers has changed considerably in the last 15 years. You can now get machines small enough to sit on the corner of your desk as well as a wide range of stand-alone models.

Virtually all modern copiers (even desktop models) are of the 'plain paper' or 'xerographic' type. These machines use ordinary office bond quality paper. It is still possible to get hold of one of the old 'coated paper' machines but I would not recommend it. The paper is difficult to get and often quite expensive, is unlikely to be acceptable to your clients, can only be copied on one side and deteriorates at an alarming rate.

To decide what type of copier you should buy, you will need to determine your copying needs. This will include the number of copies you need per day (on average) and any special requirements such as reduction or enlargement, automatic double-sided copying, large runs (over 50 copies per run), a self-feeding facility and so on. In addition to the cost of the copier, you will need to consider the cost and availability of supplies (toner, paper, spare parts) and service.

At the cheaper end of the market are the desktop copiers. Beware of buying anything too cheap and simple. Many of the very simple desktop models can only take *one* photocopy at a time and you may have to replace the original each time you take a copy. These copiers are unlikely to be suitable for a word-processing service. On the other hand, you can now get compact desktop models which can produce multiple copies (usually up to 99 at a time) in a range of sizes for between £400 and £1000. The Selex 55, for example, produces 15 copies per minute and can handle every type of paper from A5 to A3.

Virtually all stand-alone models print multiple copies and use a range of paper sizes. You will pay more for a machine that can also reduce/enlarge, sort, collate or print in colour. Although a brand new stand-alone model may be very expensive to buy, you can hire photocopiers or get good second-hand or reconditioned models. Xerox, for example, lease photocopiers and provide a good service/maintenance back-up; Xerox also have a wide range of cheaper reconditioned models for hire or sale.

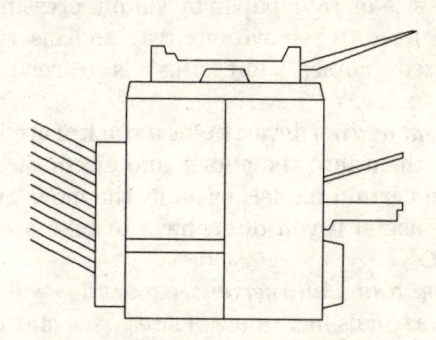

Free-standing photocopier with document feeder, choice of paper trays and collater

If you regularly need to take more than one copy from any one original, you may need a copier that can take *multiple copies*. On some models, you can set the copy counter, push the start button and wait for your copies. On others, although advertised as taking 'multiple copies', you have to reinsert the original for each additional copy. This defeats the object of having a multiple-copy machine to some extent, since you cannot leave the machine and get on with something else while your photocopies are being made. Some models leave the original in place but only take one copy at a time: you have to push the print button for every copy. If you make more single copies than anything else, one of these simpler, and usually cheaper, models will suit your purpose. However, for a few hundred pounds more, you might be able to purchase a machine which will be of greater use to your business in the *future*.

If you want to be able to make copies of books or other bulky items, you will need to have a *lift-top* model. On some models, you feed your original in one side and it is ejected, with the copy at the other. Other models have a lift-up top and a glass plate on which the original has to be placed prior to printing.

Two-sided printing saves paper and is useful for leaflets and for reducing bulk. Most plain paper copiers can print on both sides of the paper manually (you have to turn the sheets over and reinsert them the other way up) but some do it automatically. Automatic double-sided copying is usually an expensive option that you can do without.

Many copiers (including some desktop models) allow you to take *multiple-size copies*, usually A3 and A4. Some have two paper trays which hold paper of different sizes, allowing you to change the size of your paper by simply pressing a button; on others, you have to remove one tray and insert the other for different-sized copies, but this is rarely a significant disadvantage.

A *document feeding* device holds a stack of originals, automatically feeds them into the copier and ejects them. This is only available on certain models (usually the more expensive ones) but can be useful if you often have to take a copy of a large manuscript.

Reduction and enlargement capacities will allow you to reproduce originals in a range of sizes. This may be useful if you need to reduce tables or diagrams for dissertation students, or if you need to enlarge documents or graphics for use on posters or for the partially sighted.

Most copiers incorporate a feature which allows you to select an appropriate exposure setting for the work so that you can get similar results from a very dark, normal or very pale original. They usually have a range of indicators which tell you when the machine is 'warmed up' and ready for use, when you need to add paper and if there is a paper jam or other problem. Other controls generally include a dial or digital display showing the unlikely to be a very useful system for a word-processing service, even if you are only providing audio-typing for one client, because only one of you can have the machine at a time. If your client has a machine for dictation, you cannot use it for transcription: when your client returns the machine to you for transcription, he no longer has a facility for dictation! Either buy a machine that uses standard cassettes and let your customers provide their own facilities for recording, or invest in a system that uses portable dictating machines, usually with mini-cassettes, which you can provide for your clients, and a compatible transcriber which remains on your premises. If *you* provide the tapes for your customers, make sure that you erase them before sending them out again.

The operation of a transcribing machine is very straightforward. You insert your customer's pre-recorded tape and rewind to the beginning. After setting up your word processor, you press the pedal to play the tape and listen to the recording through the headset. You release the pedal to key in what you have just heard and press again to listen to some more. The system automatically backs up a little when you release the pedal so that you don't miss words when you begin typing again.

Unfortunately, the cost of new dictation equipment is quite high, around £70-£90 for a pocket memo machine, and £200-£300 for the transcription unit, foot control and headset plus the cost of cassettes. However, a lot of these machines can be purchased second-hand (watch the press for office equipment sales and auctions) and are usually perfectly serviceable.

Telephone answering machines

Once your business is established, you may find that you are constantly interrupted by customers on the telephone. This reduces your efficiency and can be an irritation when you are trying to get an urgent assignment completed. You may also be losing custom while you are out because there is no one to answer the telephone. Your regular customers are unlikely to be put off by an answering machine, especially if they know that you will get back to them quickly, but it would not be very wise to use one all the time. A potential new customer calling to enquire about your service will probably try elsewhere if met by an answering machine (and it has to be admitted that some people just do not like them). A telephone answering machine can also be useful if you are offering a phone-and-type service or a telephone answering service (see Chapter 8).

The operation of the machine is very simple. You record a

message on to a cassette tape and when you connect the machine up, this is played to callers automatically. Callers can be invited to leave a message which is recorded on another tape for you to listen to later.

Responding to the messages recorded on the machine is important. Make sure that you listen to the message tape every day (or whenever you use it) and deal promptly with any messages. One disadvantage of a telephone answering machine is that many of your customers will ask you to call them back. And this means that *you* will have to pay for the phone call.

The simplest telephone answering machines can be purchased for under £50. You should be able to buy a more sophisticated model plus a telephone and bypass monitor (which allows you to hear the caller before you decide to speak) ready to plug into your existing telephone socket for under £100.

Small items

How much additional equipment you buy will be determined by your needs and your pocket. Larger items such as telephone answering machines, copiers, transcribers, word processors and so on have already been dealt with. However, you will also need several small items of equipment if your service is to run smoothly and easily.

A hole-punch will be useful for your own filing and when your customers request that documents are punched ready for filing. Buy a strong office-duty punch with at least two hole settings and as large a gap for paper insertion as possible. It can be frustrating to have to punch a sheaf of papers in two batches because your hole-punch will not take more than two or three sheets at a time. A hole-punch that has guide markings to show you where to position the paper is very useful, especially if you have to punch many pages accurately. A good, heavy gauge, two-hole punch capable of taking about 40 sheets will cost you about £10-£15.

A stapler is another essential piece of equipment. You may already have a small pocket stapler but this is unlikely to be suitable for your purposes. In general, the larger the stapler the greater the number of sheets of paper you can fasten together with it. Choose a sturdy model that has rubber grips on the bottom (so that you don't scratch your desk and it doesn't slip while you're stapling) and make sure that you can get staples for it locally - preferably in large boxes. A hand-stapler should suffice but if you are likely to be doing *very* large amounts of stapling, you might need to consider buying an electrically powered model. These are very quick and can staple more sheets together than hand-staplers but they are rather expensive – don't buy one unless you absolutely need to. If you are producing lots of leaflets, a swivel-arm stapler which can staple along a centre fold will be useful. These can be purchased from about £20. A straightforward hand-stapler should not cost you more than about £15.

You will also find a copy-holder a boon. These come in a variety of shapes and sizes and are usually adjustable so that the work is supported at a height and angle that is easy to read without having to turn your head very far or lean over. Copy-holders with either a desk stand or an extension arm that clamps to the edge of the desk can be purchased for £10–£30. Most models have a movable cursor (sometimes magnifying) which can be moved up and down the copy according to your current typing line.

A lockable box in which to keep petty cash and stamps is also a good idea, as this will ensure you keep your business monies separate from your personal funds. Petty cash boxes can be purchased relatively cheaply from most stationers and office suppliers.

Another non-essential but highly recommended and fairly cheap item is a pocket calculator. If you are working for accountants or business people, they may want you to perform some calculations for them or check figures before typing. Even

Desktop calculator with print-out

if you don't need a calculator for your work, you will find your own bookkeeping, invoicing and estimating quicker and easier if you use a calculator. You can get a simple model that will perform basic functions (addition, subtraction, multiplication and division) for a few pounds. If you are doing a significant number of calculations for customers, you might need to invest in a larger desktop calculator that produces a print-out. Don't buy one of these until you are sure that you really need it – the cheapest models start at about £25 and perform only basic functions as well as producing a print-out.

Apart from having a place to store supplies of paper, ribbons and so on, you may need to have a readily accessible supply on or near your workstation. A small paper-holder which can be fitted to one wall or stand on the corner of your desk is very useful. These usually have several 'shelves' and can hold a small supply of paper, carbon paper (if you use it), envelopes, customers' headed paper, invoices and so on.

You may require other small items such as a waste bin, Sellotape dispenser, postage scale (buy an electronic kitchen scale – it will be cheaper!), bulletin board, scissors, staple remover, disk-storage box, spare disks and so on. All of this equipment can be purchased at stationers or office suppliers. Make a list of your needs and compare the prices and models available in several shops before you decide on your purchases. And remember to keep all your receipts.

A checklist of start-up supplies is given at the end of this chapter. You may not need to buy all of these items: beware of making unnecessary or rash purchases of equipment you may never need to use. I once decided to improve my leaflet production service by investing in a second-hand folding and stapling machine I saw advertised. The machine cost £150 (several years ago) and worked perfectly well; however, I only used it three times in three years and it never repaid its cost!

Hiring or leasing equipment

Leasing word-processing and computing equipment is a good alternative to buying if you want to spread the cost of capital outlays or upgrade frequently. It is also a way by which you can try out various systems before committing yourself fully.

Many firms now deal exclusively with the leasing of computer hardware and software, and their rates are competitive. You should be able to get a high-grade hard-disk PC, printer, maintenance and software for under £10 per week. Most firms also offer short-term rentals (one day to three months) in addition to flexible upgrading as required and full maintenance support.

You can get free quotes from: Hard-Soft International, 1a The Square, Sawbridgeworth, Herts CM21 9AE (0279 600427); Rent-IT (Europe) Limited, 10A Robin Hood Road, Woking Surrey CU21 1SP (0483 750754); and Dataline Technology, National Computer Hire & Sales, 501 Triumph House, 189 Regent Street, London W1 (0836 212209: central control), among others. Also try Yellow Pages for local leasing agents.

Renewable supplies

Renewable supplies include all the things that will be 'used up' by your word-processing service (and should be allowed for in your pricing structure). Although you will want to have an adequate range and quantity of supplies to deal with your work-load, you should not make the mistake of purchasing in bulk too soon. Start off with a small stock and increase it if you find that you are using it up too quickly.

Buy your paper in reams (500 sheets) rather than smaller quantities as it is much cheaper. Start off with one ream of a good quality A4 general typing paper: Croxley Script 85 g/m^2 is very suitable. You may also need a ream of white or coloured bank if you are going to have 'flimsy' copies, and it is a good idea to have a ream of 80 g/m^2 copier paper (not the shiny surfaced variety) for drafts. Copier paper is about half the price of 'proper' typing paper but is very similar in quality and perfectly adequate for drafts and carbon copies. If you have a dot-matrix printer (which will probably have both tractor and pin-feed mechanisms), you may also want to consider purchasing a supply of perforated continuous paper for drafts. This is cheap and can save a lot of time in hand feeding paper into the printer if you don't have an automatic cut-sheet feeder.

If you will be producing CVs or typing 'executive' letters using your own paper, you may also need to invest in a small quantity of high quality paper (100 g/m^2). A full ream will be expensive but you can get it in smaller quantities. W H Smith, for example, supply a 50 sheet pack of 'Deluxe Typing Paper' for under £3. By the way, if you are asked to use a more expensive paper, you should make sure that your charges are increased sufficiently to cover the cost. It is unlikely that you will be required to use anything other than A4 (197 × 120 mm) except for legal documents or accounts, when your client may provide the correct paper for you, but a supply of A5 paper (half the size of A4) is useful for your own invoices and estimates.

You will also need a variety of envelopes in a range of standard sizes. Unless you do a lot of envelope stuffing, 200 size 110 × 200 mm (DL) and 50 size 324 × 229 mm (C4) should suffice initially. Buy other sizes and extra supplies as needed.

Carbon paper will be needed if you intend to make carbon copies. (You will need an impact printer to do this.) Carbon copies are becoming a rarity because it is relatively easy to run off as many copies as you need on your printer. However, this uses up your printer ribbon (or toner) and you may want to retain carbon copies for your own use or to reduce costs.

You will also need to purchase a supply of paper-clips (assorted sizes), staples, sticky tape, printer ribbons, correction fluid (plus thinner), a rubber, pens, pencils (and sharpener), a ruler, jotters (you can make these yourself using the clean side of draft paper), postage stamps (first and second class to start with) and rubber bands. Buy all of these things in small quantities at first and build up supplies as your work-load increases. Do remember to get and keep receipts for everything and write these purchases in your cash book straight away.

Checklist of start-up supplies

The following checklist is for guidance only: it is highly unlikely that you will need or want to purchase all the things on this list. Use it selectively. Space has been left for you to include any other items you might need. Tailor your requirements to suit your own service, needs and financial constraints. Shop around for the best value. Adding on any other initial expenses (eg advertising launch, printing business cards or office decoration) will give you a good ideal of your initial costs.

Tools of the Trade

	£		£
Desk/workstation	....	Calculator	....
Filing cabinet	....	Dictionary	....
Shelving	....	Thesaurus	....
WP/computer	....	Waste bin	....
Printer	....	Stapler	....
Typewriter	....	Software	....
Photocopier	....	Hole-punch	....
Answering machine	....	Petty cash box	....
Dictation equipment	....	Sellotape (and dispenser)	....
Telephone	....	Manilla folders	....
Typist's chair	....	Sample display book	....
Facsimile machine	....		

Others:

....	....	Ring binders	....
....	....	Accounts books	....
....	....	Desk diary	....
....	....	Report binders	....
....	....	Paper	....
....	....	Envelopes	....
....	....	Carbon paper	....
....	....	Ribbons/toner	....
....	....	Address book (or card index)	....
....	....	Disks and disk box	....
....	....	Copy-holder	....
....	....	Sundries: paper-clips, pens, rubber bands, postage stamps, jotters etc	....

TOTAL START-UP COSTS   £ _____

Chapter 7
Daily Operation of the Business

Organising your time

Lack of organisation is one of the major time-wasters of any business. It is anathema to a home-based word-processing service. For you, time *is* money. If you work inefficiently, are constantly interrupted, have to spend hours sorting out materials before you can begin an assignment, or find that your customers spend half the day at your house drinking coffee, you need to organise your time better!

When you first start your word-processing service, you may encounter time management problems. Among them, determining how much work you can deal with in a given time and keeping distractions (both personal and business) to a minimum will probably rate quite highly.

Because running a home-based word-processing service is such a very personalised occupation, you will have to learn from your own experience how to estimate the time needed to complete assignments and how to minimise interruptions. However, you can save yourself a lot of stress and harassment if you keep a daily time chart. On this chart, you should list your plans for the day and estimate how much time each job will take. At the end of the day, record how much time the job *actually* consumed and include a note of all the additional unexpected tasks or distractions you had to contend with during the day and how long *they* took. After a few days of doing this, you will probably find that you tend to underestimate the time required to accomplish word-processing assignments and that distractions and interruptions take up a considerable amount of your 'working' time and interfere with your planned work periods.

When you estimate the time needed to complete an assignment, don't forget to include time spent with the customer *beforehand*, time spent proof-reading, and time spent going over the completed work with the customer *afterwards*. Also make an allowance for corrections and rewording and then add extra time for possible interruptions. It is better to overestimate the time required to complete a task (leaving you with extra time for emergencies and other tasks, or just enjoying yourself) than it is to live in a permanent frenzy of activity trying to meet impossible deadlines and resenting every interruption.

Go through your time chart and find out where you are losing time. The following checklist will help you to pin-point and eliminate the major time-consuming problems.

1. Procrastination

Inevitably, there will be times when you are faced with an assignment that you know is going to be a chore and you find innumerable excuses to avoid starting it. We all procrastinate at times, but if you are working from home, this can be a particularly difficult problem: it is all too easy to put off the dreaded assignment until the last minute. Deferring unpleasant tasks may mean that the work will be rushed and perhaps badly done. If you find procrastination is often a problem, you will need to tackle it positively.

First, find out what sorts of assignment you tend to defer. Do you dislike typing tables, or envelopes? Perhaps you find it difficult to make a start on a long thesis or manuscript? Make a particular effort to deal with those problem areas. If you dislike typing tables, for example, and have a document that contains quite a few, try typing all the tables *first* while the tabs are set and you are fresh. Once they are done, you will probably be able to get through the rest of the work in double-quick time. If you dread long and complex tasks, then break them up into manageable chunks, plan a timetable for completion of each part and make yourself stick to it. In time, you should be able to tackle any assignment with confidence and ease.

2. Callers

There are two types of caller who may disrupt your routine: personal callers (family, friends, the milkman, salesmen etc) and unexpected customers. These interruptions break your concentration and take up valuable time. You will need to be particularly firm with the former. Tell them you're busy and ask them to call again at a more convenient time.

Unexpected customers are more difficult to deal with. How you tackle this will depend to some extent on how much work you have to do and whether you feel it necessary to tolerate 'drop-in' customers in order to maintain their goodwill. Unfortunately, there are some customers who tend to treat home-workers like doormats! They will turn up at weekends, at mealtimes and during the evening, never apologise for interrupting what is probably your leisure time, and expect you to drop everything in order to deal with their 'urgent' work. You may be happy to accept this sort of thing, especially in the initial stages while you are building up a work-load, but if you find it is a problem, you will have to point out tactfully that it is in your customers' best interests to *telephone* you first for an appointment. They may have a wasted journey if you are out, for example. Give them one of your business cards so that they have a note of your telephone number and write your business hours on the back for persistent offenders. It is much easier to explain to a customer that it is not convenient for them to call that evening if they are on the telephone than it is if they are standing on your doorstep!

3. Telephone calls
Look at your time chart. Do you make several telephone calls during the day all at different times? You can save yourself time and avoid 'losing the thread' of your work if you can group calls at a convenient break-point. Plan each call in advance. Prepare a list of the points you want to make and, as you ask each question, write the answer next to it on the sheet. Be brief. Once you have the information you require, end the call. Don't get caught up in socialising.

If you are constantly interrupted by people phoning you, you might consider buying or hiring an answering machine. Some people intensely dislike using these and you may therefore lose custom if you are rarely available to answer the telephone personally, but they can be a boon if you have a long and complicated assignment to complete and are constantly having to break off to answer the telephone.

When making outgoing calls, use any time while 'on hold' (a long cord and shoulder rest are good for this) to do filing, clear your desk and so on. Another useful device is a telephone with a memory and re-dial facility. These are no more expensive than an ordinary telephone (you can purchase one for less than £20). If you are trying to get a number that is engaged, you simply press a button and the number will be re-dialled automatically for you. This can be surprisingly time-saving as you can carrying on working at your keyboard while the number is dialled.

4. Underestimating the time required to complete a task
This is a very common problem in the early stages. Not only will you become more proficient as time goes on but you will also

learn better how to judge the time required to complete an assignment.

Look at the reasons *why* a particular assignment took longer to complete than expected. Did you find you had to slow down or stop because you weren't sure how your customer wanted the work done? You can avoid this by going through the work carefully with your customer beforehand. Did you have to stop to hunt for files or references? By assembling all the equipment, books and papers you need for a particular assignment before you start, you can eliminate time wasted due to disorganisation. Clear your desk of everything but the task in hand. Were you plagued by interruptions? If you can't eliminate or reduce interruptions, perhaps you could organise your schedule so that you are working on the complex assignments during the quietest period of your day and dealing with the less demanding tasks (envelope addressing, filing and so on) during your more 'disturbed' periods.

Allow extra time for keying in lots of figures, tables, bibliographies etc, or for interpreting poor handwriting or specialised terminology. Make sure that you also allow sufficient time for proof-reading, corrections and telephone calls from customers.

5. Corrections and alterations

Are corrections and alterations taking up more time that they should? Find out where your problems arise. If you are making a lot of mistakes, you are either working too fast or are not concentrating on the task in hand. Give yourself more time to complete an assignment and try to concentrate on *one* task at a time. Above all, try to *finish* one task before starting another.

Some mistakes will not be picked up by your word processor's spell-checker no matter how religiously you use it. A spell-checker will not pick up errors where an inappropriate but correctly spelled word is inserted, or where you have missed out, transposed or duplicated portions of text. For example, 'James was hear' would not be detected as incorrect. Neither would grammatical gobbledegook such as 'He went then can we have three copies!' Careful proof-reading is therefore essential. It can mean the difference between handing over a piece of work that is full of glaring errors and silly mistakes and providing a letter-perfect product.

If you find that you often miss mistakes on your own proof-reading of the work, you could ask a friend to check your printed copy while you read the original. It is better to correct any errors *before* you hand over the work to the customer for checking.

If you find that certain customers often return asking for extensive alterations, you could suggest that you prepare an initial draft for them and produce the final version after any corrections and alterations have been made. This may save on printing time (if your printer has a draft mode) and materials.

6. Priorities

Once you have got into the habit of making a list of tasks for the day, you should try to assign *priorities* to those tasks. Decide which are the most critical and do those *first*. Then, if you are delayed later on, at least you will have completed the most important assignments. Always finish one task before starting on the next. You will waste time and fail to do justice to any assignment if you constantly jump from one task to another.

7. More time-saving tips

Plan to make all your purchases of new supplies at the same time and arrange to visit the various suppliers in the most economic (in terms of time) order. Try to get suppliers to deliver your requisitions rather than having to collect them yourself. Many will be happy to do this if you are putting in a reasonably large order once a month or so. If you are likely to be delayed anywhere, take some proof-reading with you. (You can also proof-read during 'holding' time on the telephone.)

Ensure that your office and desk are organised efficiently. Keep frequently used items in your top drawers and clear away items that are rarely used. Establish a good simple filing system and *use* it. File every day. Avoid having piles of disorganised paper lying around because you don't know where to put them.

Take your post straight to your desk when it arrives, open it and decide on a plan of action for each item immediately. If writing replies, making phone calls or dealing with extra work is necessary, make a note of these at appropriate places on your day's work-plan.

8. Time for yourself

Don't get so involved in your word-processing service that you neglect your private life. You are not trying to work efficiently and eliminate time-wasting only to cram in even more work.

Try not to be overtaken by the desire to make more and more money. Inevitably, the 'pound signs' will light up in front of your eyes when a customer calls offering you work and it is *very* difficult to turn work away. Unless you are going 'all out' and are prepared to let your business grow and expand rapidly (and work 15 hours a day), you could easily be put off by taking on too much too soon. If you really want to work only eight hours a day and are already fully booked, think carefully about what you'll have to forgo if you take on extra assignments.

Dealing with customers

Handling customers, particularly your first dozen or so, can be a traumatic experience. Even if you have had a lot of practice in previous employment or have always found it easy to 'get on' with people in general, you may find your role more difficult when you become self-employed. Some people find it more difficult to adopt a businesslike manner with a customer sitting in their lounge, for example, than they would with a customer in an office or shop. Your home, in this instance, is also your place of work and, although friendly relations with your customers may be beneficial, you must bear in mind that they are not guests but business associates. An excess of small talk will waste your time (and possibly your customers') and may give the impression that you are not terribly efficient or businesslike.

Surprisingly, perhaps, your customers may have a similar problem. If you were sitting behind a counter in an office, they would probably have no trouble at all in explaining their requirements and asking for information: sitting in your *personal* lounge, drinking *your* coffee, they may feel rather less assertive and sure of themselves.

As in any business, the variety of customers you will meet is endless. Some, and particularly *other* small business owners, will already have very firm ideas about the layout, spacing, copies and format they require for their word-processing. You will be able to ascertain the needs of these customers quickly, easily and with the minimum of fuss. Others will have only the vaguest idea of what they want, what you can provide or how much information you need. With such a customer, you will need to be able to ask all the relevant questions, find out his precise needs and clearly explain how you can supply them.

Directing the conversation

In any dealings with customers, you will need to balance a friendly, helpful, interested manner with a businesslike approach that tells them you've got work to do. Be friendly but don't allow your customers to intrude on your time by spending too long chatting. If you do have this problem, which is surprisingly common, bring their attention back to the work in hand by recapping, saying something like: 'Well Mrs Smith, I'll have two copies of your report ready for you by 3 pm on Friday then. Could you leave me a note of your telephone number in case I need to contact you in the meantime?' At the same time, pick up your customer's piece of work and stand up: this will almost certainly motivate your customer to do the same. Once you've got them on their feet, walk over to the door and hold it open for them. It doesn't matter if they start chatting again at this point as they're on their way out anyway!

Customers who are side-tracked in the middle of discussing their requirements also need direction. This can be particularly difficult if your service includes an element of 'interviewing', as would be necessary for a comprehensive CV service for example. In this case, you will have to allow sufficient time (at least half an hour) for discussing layout and style, content and presentation, and for taking down all the relevant details. Remember that *you* must take the leading role. If your customer is side-tracked, *you* should bring his attention back to the work in hand. Your customers will expect you to take the lead in asking questions and proffering information.

It is much easier for both you and your customer to adopt the appropriate 'roles' if you have a room or area set aside for use as your 'office'. It may also give your customers confidence if they can see where you do the work. It can be nerve-racking for a student, for example, to leave the only copy of his precious thesis with an unknown person who simply puts it on top of the TV and goes back to making the lunch!

Telephone queries

Customers will almost invariably make the initial contact with you by telephone. Unlike a town centre agency, you will get very few new customers turning up unexpectedly at the door. You will therefore need to develop a polite and proficient telephone manner. Most customers will be telephoning several word-processing services to compare prices, so you need to be able to present *your* service as the best, if not the cheapest, available. Don't simply give your charges and leave it at that. It takes only a few seconds to ask customers what their word-processing requirements are. Emphasise your ability to provide the particular service your customer is looking for – a fast turnaround, a guarantee of accuracy, free copies, correction of grammar and spelling, collection/delivery or whatever – *before* you tell them what your charges are. Be helpful and positive. Perhaps you could offer to send them a sample of a leaflet outlining your service and charges. This gives you a good opportunity to 'get your foot in the door' with a potential customer, even if they don't use you on this occasion.

Keep your appointments book (a diary will do) and a 'work in hand' journal by the telephone so that you can decide on your ability to meet a commitment while you're speaking to the customer. Potential customers might be put off if you give the impression that you aren't sure whether you can fit in a piece of work or not, or if you have to leave them waiting on the line while you rummage about trying to find your appointments book.

There will be occasions when a new potential customer calls with some urgent work when you are fully booked. To some extent, you need to be guided by your own judgement in these circumstances. If the customer is a small business person who may well decide to use your services regularly, you may wish to put in some extra time with a view to securing future custom; likewise, you may want to fit in a regular user in order to maintain his goodwill. On the other hand, the customer may require a large one-off word-processing assignment (eg a dissertation) and/or you may find it impossible to fit in the work. If this is the case, don't simply tell the caller that you cannot do the work: apologise and explain that you are fully booked at the time, offer to send a leaflet outlining your service and charges for future use, and if possible provide the caller with another contact (perhaps another home-based service you know of) who may be able to help. Hopefully, your caller will be impressed enough either to try you again in the future or to pass on your name to some other potential customer.

Dealing with several customers at once

During your working day, you will also have customers calling at your home to collect or deliver work. For most of these, you will have made an appointment, but many customers (especially regulars) will call without telephoning in advance. The fact that your customers may fail to keep to the time of an agreed appointment or may call on spec means that you will, on some occasions, have several customers on your premises at once. This should not be a problem as long as you can keep the customer you are dealing with at that time separate from the others. Most customers expect – even require – a degree of confidentiality in their dealings with you and may not be too happy if they have to discuss their requirements or check work in the presence of others.

Here again, a separate office in which you can go over the work with customers is the best situation. You can then leave unexpected callers in the comfort of your lounge while you attend to each customer individually in your interview area.

Ascertaining the customers' needs
One of your major aims when dealing with customers will be to find out what they want done and to provide them with information about deadlines, charges, corrections, alterations and so on.

When your customer brings you an assignment, take time to go through it carefully with him *while he is there*. Be sure to ask about the kind of paper required, line spacing, margins, whether paragraphs should be indented, how the work should be laid out and so on. Does your customer want a particular typeface and point size (fount)? Do customers want carbon copies, photocopies or additional printed copies, and how many? Do they want you to produce a draft first for checking? Also, make sure that you get a telephone number where you can contact them if need be. Obviously, you don't want to ring unnecessarily with queries, but you *may* have to.

If there are insertions and alterations on the copy, are these clearly marked? Any insertions should (preferably) be marked 1, 2, 3 and so forth, in a bold colour with an arrow showing where in the text they are to be inserted. The text to be inserted should be numbered correspondingly and written on a separate sheet. Deletions should be crossed out with a single clear line. Any supplementary information about layout, paragraphing and so on should be written in a different-coloured ink from the actual text – although it is, of course, easier for you if the only writing on a page is that which you have to type! Unfortunately, you will receive many badly written texts covered with unintelligible corrections and deletions and with little notes (to you) written all over them! If you are presented with an extensive document which has been substantially altered without any consistency, you could offer to prepare an initial draft (for an extra charge, of course) which can then be used as a basis for any further alteration.

Bad handwriting
Perhaps the biggest bugbear of the typist or WP operator is bad handwriting. Unless the writing is really terrible (or, worse, inconsistent), you should be able to interpret it as long as the sentences are grammatically correct and of a non-technical nature. However, make sure that customers with poor handwrit-

ing print out personal names, place names and all technical, scientific, legal and medical words clearly (preferably above the handwritten word).

Don't be afraid to say that the handwriting is difficult to understand if it is. Most people already know if their handwriting is awful and won't be offended. Only on one occasion has a customer been taken aback by my comment that I found the handwriting a problem. She had a very 'decorative', almost gothic, style of writing which many people had told her looked splendid. It did. But it was *very* difficult to read! Another regular customer not only had the most terrible handwriting I've ever seen but never finished a sentence (except in his head!). Every single sentence tailed off into a wriggling line so that the last half-dozen words were open to pure guesswork. Fortunately, he realised he had a problem and was so pleased to have someone who would even attempt to interpret his scrawls that he was happy to pay double the normal rate plus an allowance for preparing a draft version each time!

If you think the handwriting or presentation is likely to slow you down, tell your customer in advance that your charge may be slightly higher because the work may take longer than normal to complete. Don't shock your customer by asking for substantially more than was expected when he comes to collect the work.

Remembering the customers' instructions

While you are going through the work with customers, make sure that you attend to what they are saying. Don't be reading the bottom of the page if they are explaining something at the top. Most important of all, make a note of the customers' instructions immediately and check these over with them again before they leave. Don't put it off until later. When you have several different assignments going at the same time, it is all too easy to forget whether customer A wanted two or three copies on 80 g/m^2 white or whether customer B asked you to print addresses at the bottom or top of letters.

It is an excellent idea to have a set of pre-printed forms available for completion while you are interviewing the customer. You can print one of these yourself and have 50 or so photocopies produced. Save a copy of the form on disk and run off batches as and when you need them. These should have details of the customer's name, address and telephone number(s) together with a summary of the work, any special requirements, the agreed deadline, charging policy adopted and

SUSIE'S SECRETARIAL SERVICES

Word-processing service work-form

Customer's details: Name: ....
   Address: ....
   ....
   ....
   Telephone (Home): ....
   (Work): ....

Details of work required:
....
....
....
....

No of copies: ....   Type of copy: ....
Spacing: ....   Margins: ....
Indentation: ....   Headings: ....
Paper: ....
Fount details: ....
Special requirements: ....
....
Collection date and time: ....

Price:

Estimated cost: £....................................   Actual cost: £....................................
   Copies: £....................................
   Postage: £....................................
   Phone calls: £....................................
   Alterations: £....................................
   Others: £....................................
   TOTAL £....................................

Invoice no: ....   Receipt no: ....

Notes:

the estimated cost. An example is shown on page 124. You can adapt this idea to suit your own requirements.

A properly completed form is an indispensable reference to remind you of the customer's requirements and it can be usefully integrated into your record-keeping system. The form can be filed in your 'work in hand' file initially, affixed to the appropriate copy invoice when the work has been completed, and the whole lot attached to your copy receipt when the job has been paid for. You can transfer details to your cash book directly from the form.

Another advantage of such a form is that you can use it to retain full details of the work you have done for a particular customer. This can be extremely useful when that customer calls to request further work because you will have a note of your previous charging policy, how quickly the customer paid, whether the work took longer than expected and why, any problems you had and so on.

Alterations, corrections and mistakes

However good a typist you are, you will on occasion make mistakes. There will also be times when you will be asked to make alterations because your *customer* has made a mistake or has decided to reword something. Alterations are endemic to some assignments. Masters' and doctoral theses, for example, normally have to be redone at least once after submission for preliminary checking. Assuming you have a word processor, this is no problem, since the bulk of the text, which you will have stored on disk, will remain the same; you will only have to carry out the alterations. Using a conventional typewriter, you may have to retype the whole lot. This can be a very long job – such theses are usually somewhere between 10,000 and 80,000 words long – so you should charge accordingly.

Charging for changes

One of the questions frequently asked by the owners of new word-processing services is: 'Should I charge for corrections?' A reasonable policy to adopt is: if a mistake is *yours*, correct it free of charge; if a mistake is the *customer's*, charge him.

Charging customers for mistakes can be problematical if you don't charge an hourly rate. The simplest approach is probably to go through the alterations with the customer, explain that you will have to charge him for them and then give a reasonable estimate of the price depending on the extent of reworking required. This approach is usually most acceptable to the customer. Obviously, you will have to modify your policy in the light of the amount of actual work and expense the alterations will involve. A single alteration on every page of a long text will clearly have to be charged for since you will have to run off the whole document again, whereas you may decide *not* to charge for several alterations (or one changed paragraph say) that affect only a single page and will take you only five minutes to do.

Who is to blame?

Problems can arise when the customer feels that he *has* given you the correct instructions but you have interpreted them wrongly. This is to be avoided at all costs! Careful notes on your work-form should help but occasionally customers do not fully understand what is meant by 'indentation', 'block paragraphs', 'bold type', '10 point' and so on, and are unpleasantly surprised by the appearance of the finished product.

Samples showing a variety of typefaces, point sizes and formats as well as the various accepted methods of punctuation, page continuation, numbering and so on, can eliminate this problem. It is rarely a good idea to allow a customer to say 'Oh, you lay it out the way you think it should be' or 'You're the expert, I'll leave that to you'. When they see the finished product, they may change their minds! If you are asked for advice, by all means give it. That is, after all, part of your service. But make sure that the customer understands exactly *how* you intend to present the work. Show samples to clarify your proposals and ensure that your customer agrees with these.

Proof-reading

It is better to have a time gap between keying-in and proof-reading, as it can be remarkably difficult to spot your own errors shortly after you have finished a piece of work. Some people can cope with proof-reading 'on screen' while others hardly ever spot mistakes this way! If you have this problem, it is better to run off a paper copy for proof-checking.

For longer papers or those with a lot of numbers, you will find proof-reading easier if you can get someone to read the printed copy while you read the original out loud. If you are a fast reader, you may find accurate proof-reading particularly difficult because you will be used to reading groups of words at a glance. For good proof-reading, you need to re-train yourself to read individual *letters* in the words. Make a conscious effort to slow yourself down. If you find yourself running ahead, use a ruler or piece of paper with a slot cut in it to fix your attention on one line or group of words at a time.

When you find a mistake, make a note of it immediately and mark a prominent cross in the margin to attract your attention to it later. You can then reload the saved document, make the corrections required and run off a perfect copy of the pages required.

Common errors
Apart from simple spelling mistakes, common typing errors include repeating double letters, missing out letters in a word (especially in long words), substituting one correctly spelled word for another ('there' for 'their'), missing out chunks of text, breaks in continuity between one page and the next, repeating or missing out words, faulty punctuation and errors in keying-in numbers. Only the first three types of errors will be picked up by the spell-check program on your word processor.

It is particularly easy to omit a section or paragraph especially if it starts with the same word or phrase as the next. Repeating letters, as in the words 'confidentialiity' and 'controllling', is another common error, difficult to detect without a spell-checker. Beware of other hard-to-spot mistakes such as typing 'affect' for 'effect' (or vice versa), transposing letters (for example, typing 'reciept' for 'receipt') or missing out letters (for example, typing 'satelite' instead of 'satellite'). Possibly the most easily overlooked errors lie in small words, with only one letter difference, such as it/is/in/if, or/on, as/at and so on.

Certain words have alternative forms of spelling (equally correct) but your customer may have a preference. Find out what it is and be consistent. Examples are:

> realise/realize (-ise or -ize ending)   grey/gray
> adviser/advisor   despatch/dispatch
> medieval/mediaeval   carcass/carcase

Flexibility – go with your customers

When you first start your word-processing service, you may want to take on any kind of work you can get. This is a good way to find out what market there is in your area: something that is difficult to predict in advance.

Adopting a flexible approach is probably essential in the early stages. Even if you ultimately intend to specialise, you will almost certainly need to diversify initially. A specialist service usually takes time to build up. Your eventual goal, for instance, may be to work exclusively for a number of small businesses in the area. There is nothing wrong with this idea: once you have an established network of customers, your advertising costs will be low, you will 'know' your customers, and the work should be predictable and, hopefully, fairly regular. However, you won't achieve a full work-load of this sort immediately. It may take up to a year of continual advertising and regular mail shots to attract a sufficient, suitable, work supply.

There are disadvantages in specialising. If you work almost exclusively for a few established customers, for example, it can be very difficult to take holidays, reduce or increase your work-load for any reason, or avoid periods of over- or under-work.

Consider the following example. Your service is geared to the secretarial work of 10 small businesses and you also take seasonal overflow work from two large organisations. One of the big firms phones you because they have 1000 invoices to be prepared by the following week. Since you are in a slack period, you agree to take the work on. Later that day, two of your small firms phone to ask you to prepare 20 letters and a 200-page bill of quantities (you cannot refuse either since they both have retainer contracts with you). The following day, another two of your small businesses want you to type 300 envelopes and 15 sets of accounts respectively. You suddenly find yourself working from 6 am to 11 pm every day!

This won't always happen, of course. Most of the time you will probably have a regular, steady, supply of work. The point is, if you have this kind of arrangement, you may forgo control over how much, how little or what you do. So think about the disadvantages as well as the advantages of such a situation.

You can often maintain greater flexibility, and will certainly have to deal with a broader variety of people and assignments, if you retain an open approach. The disadvantages of flexibility are that your work-load may be more irregular, you will probably have to advertise more widely and frequently, you will have to deal with more new customers, you will need a wider range of skills and you may suffer from more bad debts. On the other hand, you will have little difficulty in turning work away when it suits you, taking holidays and expanding or reducing your work-load as you wish. You will also have the intellectual satisfaction and stimulation of dealing with a great variety of assignments and meeting lots of new people.

For the many home-based word-processing services who adopt the flexible approach, their work-load often has a seasonal variability. The bulk of dissertations and theses, for example, will come towards the end of the college or university term; large organisations often tend to release special Christmas promotions and bulk mailings in December; accountants are usually swamped with tax computations, accounts and tax returns during March and April, and so on.

During these peak periods, you are likely to be overrun with work; in fact, you may wish to take on temporary staff or subcontractors (see Chapter 9), but at other times you will need to ensure that you have sufficient non-seasonal work to keep you going.

You will need to gear your advertising appropriately to capture the 'peak' markets and to have a good supply of customers waiting 'in the wings' during your infill periods. Don't wait until you run out of work to start advertising for more. Plan well in advance. About a fortnight before you think one of your seasonal 'flushes' will end, you should be advertising for your next batch of customers. You will learn from experience what type of promotion achieves the best results for you.

By following the requirements of your customers, your word-processing service will be able to develop and to grow to its full potential, *you* will remain in charge of what you do and when you do it, and you will be able to maintain and develop an immense range of skills which will stand you in good stead for the future.

Daily money matters

Cash or cheque

Money will flow through your business via your petty cash box and your business bank account. You can, of course, use a personal bank account for business receipts and payments but, as mentioned in Chapter 4, this *may* cause problems if you need to prove the state of your business banking for tax purposes.

Keep a good supply of change in your petty cash box. This will be useful for small purchases and particularly necessary when you need to give change to customers. A £30 float should suffice.

For relatively small jobs, your customers will probably pay in cash, but they may want to pay by cheque for larger, more expensive, assignments. Accepting a cheque imposes some risk on you but you can minimise this by following these guide-lines:

1. Only accept a personal cheque if the customer has a cheque guarantee card to support it. Even students can normally get these from their banks. Otherwise insist on cash.

2. Check the following details on the cheque: the date, your name (or business name if you have a separate account), the words and figures agree, and the cheque has been signed (in your presence).
3. Check the following details on the card: the expiry date (it should not have run out), the signature matches the one on the cheque, the code numbers on the card and cheque are the same (the code number is not the *card* number), and the cheque guarantee card covers the value of the cheque (usually up to £50 or up to £100).
4. Ensure that the cheque is for £50 (or £100 if the customer has a £100 cheque guarantee card) or under. If the bill is for more than this amount, ask your customer for further identification (something with another signature, name and address on it) and take a note of his full address. The bank only 'guarantees' to pay a cheque up to the value shown on the cheque guarantee card; if the cheque is for more than this and your customer has insufficient funds in his account, his bank may refuse to pay you. Some people ask for more than one cheque in these circumstances but banks can also refuse to pay out on two cheques (both under £50) which they believe to be for the same transaction. Providing separate invoices may overcome this problem.
5. Most cheque cards have the account holder's name printed on them. Make sure that this is your customer's name. If in any doubt, ask to see some further identification such as a driver's licence, passport, or child benefit or pension book.
6. Write the card number (this will have the words 'card number' written underneath it) on the back of the cheque.
7. Ensure that you have the customer's correct name and address in case of any query. You should already have this if you fully completed one of your work-forms at the outset.
8. Pay cheques into your bank account as soon as possible.

Credit cards

An alternative to accepting payment by either cash or cheque is to offer a credit card facility. You must have a separate business bank account and you need to hire (or buy) an imprinting machine. The credit card companies will provide the sales slips. You simply bank your copies of these slips and, at the end of the month, the credit card company totals your sales for the month and charges you a small percentage for providing the service. (You might consider building this charge into your quotations.)

The advantage of accepting credit cards for payment is that provided the card hasn't expired, isn't defaced and isn't on your list of stolen cards (issued by your bank), you can't be held liable for bad debts. It is up to the credit card company to get the money from the customer; you will already have been paid. Ask your bank for further information on this facility.

When should the customer pay?
When the customer pays for your service will depend on the following:

(a) The type and cost of the job.
(b) The status of the customer.
(c) The agreement between you.

For small one-off jobs, such as the production of a few letters, you should expect payment upon the customer's receipt or collection of the finished work. Give customers time to go through the work on your premises so that they are satisfied that it is correct before being asked for payment.

If you operate your business mainly on a postal system, you will either have to adopt a policy of asking for a deposit (or full payment) in advance or invoice customers when you return the finished product to them. If you elect to invoice customers, state your terms on the invoice ('please pay immediately', '30 days net' or whatever).

Business customers will often pay a quarterly retaining fee and expect to be invoiced for any actual work done (probably monthly). You will send out your quarterly retaining fee invoice every three months (about a month before it is due for renewal) and other invoices on a regular basis. Large organisations may have a long and complicated payment procedure, but if you have to wait longer than 28 days, send out a reminder (or statement) and phone the client to find out why you have not been paid.

It is generally better (and normally expected) that 'personal' customers, such as writers, students and job-seekers, should pay *immediately* upon receipt of the finished work. Unless your customer is a regular user of your service, or you are otherwise *certain* you will be paid, it is rarely a good idea to give credit to such customers. If your customers arrive and 'suddenly' find they can't pay you on the spot, it would be quite reasonable to refuse to let them take the work away, especially if it is an expensive job. Explain that it is your policy to retain the work until payment is made and suggest that they arrange to call again later with the money and collect the work then.

Occasionally, you will do an extensive piece of work for a personal customer which cannot reasonably be checked 'on the spot' (a book or play script, for example). If the customer wants to take the work away for checking and is concerned about paying you the full amount before the work is checked, ask for a substantial deposit and allow the customer to take only one copy away. You should also ask for identification to confirm the customer's name and address in case of future difficulties. Make definite arrangements for the collection of further copies/payment of the outstanding sum and confirm your correction/alteration policy with the customer before he leaves.

Some services, especially personal postal ones, such as the preparation and production of a CV, are normally paid for in advance. If you charge customers in advance for such a service, make sure that you explain that the money will be refunded if the customer is dissatisfied and returns everything to you within a certain period (normally within 10 days to a fortnight). You might also like to ask for an advance deposit on a very large job, especially if it is for a new customer.

Paying your creditors

Many of your day-to-day purchases will be on a cash basis; that is, you will pay for the goods (stamps, paper, ribbons etc) and services (photocopying, printing) as you buy them. Once you are established, you may be able to set up credit arrangements with your major suppliers, who will then invoice you for the purchases. This is obviously better for *you* because you don't have to take money out of your business straight away.

If you have several creditors and lessors, you should have a properly organised system of payment which ensures that you neither pay unnecessarily early, nor invariably put off payments until you receive the final demand. You want to retain the goodwill of your creditors and you should not subject them to the nuisances you yourself are trying to avoid.

Check the financial state of your word-processing service regularly, not just when the annual accounts are prepared. Make sure that you have sufficient funds to pay your creditors (even if you don't *actually* pay them until later). Are you *owed* more money by debtors that *you* owe to creditors? What would happen to your business if your debtors decided not to pay you? Would you still be solvent? Once you are dealing with invoiced customers and are paying for your supplies on credit, you need to be especially careful about watching your cash flow. Things can easily get out of hand.

A checklist to help your word-processing service run smoothly

- Keep a daily work chart to find out where you are losing or wasting time. Once you have isolated your problem areas, take positive action to eliminate or reduce them.
- Assign priorities to your work and always complete one task before beginning another.
- Allow plenty of time to complete an assignment. Remember to allow for proof-reading, corrections and interruptions.
- Do not postpone important matters that are unpleasant. They will block your brain and reduce your creativity and working capacity. Do the unpleasant things first, then the rest of the day will be easy.
- Don't allow family and friends to intrude on your working time.
- Group telephone calls. Plan calls in advance. Separate *chat* from information. Keep an egg-timer by the phone (or get a phone that shows you how long you have been on a call). Get an answering machine if you are constantly interrupted by telephone calls.
- Don't take on more work that you can handle.
- Compile a list of other typists/WP operators who can help occasional overloads.
- Prepare a set of work-forms tailored to your own service and requirements.
- File daily. Deal with post straight away.
- Keep your desk clear of everything but the assignment in hand.
- Set up a contact and customer file (an address book or index cards will do) detailing names, addresses and telephone numbers of your clients and contacts.
- Change printer/typewriter ribbons after every 30–35 pages of text. Check the last page printed against the *first* page printed to see if it's time to change. Keep old ribbons for drafts and unimportant jobs (or re-inking).
- Proof-read carefully. Use a ruler or guide to focus your attention, or read aloud to another person.
- Always get a telephone number where you can contact your customer if you run into difficulties. Let the customer know as soon as possible if you cannot meet a deadline.

- Advertise well in advance of your need for more work.
- Go through the work carefully with customers before they leave. Make sure that *you* understand their requirements and that *they* are aware of your pricing/alteration/correction policies.
- Make time to go through your records regularly (once a month when you total your cash book is a good time). Is your service doing as well as you predicted? Are you having any problems with debtors/creditors?
- Above all, *enjoy* your word-processing service. You will not do your business justice if you are doing it half-heartedly or find the pressures difficult to cope with. Put *yourself* in your daily schedule.

Chapter 8
New Horizons: Expanding into New Fields

Running a home-based word-processing service doesn't necessarily mean restricting yourself to straightforward word-processing at home. There is an almost endless range of additional services you can offer which will enhance and improve your business. Supplementary services you might like to consider are outlined in this chapter.

Photocopying

As well as relieving you of the need to print additional copies, photocopying can be offered as a separate facility to your customers. A great many people need to have photocopies made whether or not they also require word-processing and, provided your location is convenient and your rates are reasonable, you should be able to attract customers purely on the basis of a photocopying service.

Collection and delivery

This is one of the commonest extras offered by home-based word-processing services for good reason. Unless you live in the centre of town or on a major road, you will probably be somewhat out of the way for your customers. This is not likely to be a severe hindrance. However, you will undoubtedly broaden the range of potential customers if you can offer to collect work and deliver at their convenience.

This service can be especially useful for other small businesses who often do not have the *time* to travel to and from a secretarial agency delivering and collecting work.

Apart from enhancing your service in the eyes of your customers, collection and delivery has other advantages. You can reduce the number of drop-in customers and have more control over how long you spend chatting to them. (It is easier to finalise dealings if *you* have to leave *their* premises than if you have to extricate them from yours!) On the other hand, the time you spend travelling uses fuel (or pedal power) and takes up your time. In addition, you are not at home to take telephone calls or to carry on with other assignments.

You will have to make a financial assessment of the cost of providing the service. Allow for petrol, wear and tear on the car, and your travelling time. For short runs, you may simply want to include the cost of collection and delivery in the price of the work, but make a charge for longer (or frequent) journeys. Whether you are providing a free service to attract custom or are making a charge (either at cost or for profit) for it, you should know how much the service is actually costing *you*. Remember to allow for these costs in your annual accounts and in your day-to-day cash flow forecasting.

'Mobile' secretary

Providing a mobile secretarial service is quite different from working at home. Apart from slightly different equipment needs (you will need a portable electric typewriter or word processor and printer, a telephone and a car), you will be working predominantly on other people's premises, probably using their stationery and doing a wider range of secretarial jobs (filing, drafting letters, taking shorthand, making bookings, bookkeeping and so on) than you would working from home. You will almost certainly want to charge by the hour for a service of this kind. Your charges will need to take into account travelling costs, any materials you have to provide, and wear and tear on your portable equipment. Some of your costs may be lower because you will be using your customer's heat, light, electricity, furniture and premises.

This kind of service is relatively rare although there *is* a demand for it. In rural areas especially, farmers and landowners may be delighted to have someone to do the office work once a week. They certainly won't have the time to bring the work to you. There are also innumerable businesses with insufficient secretarial needs to employ staff, even on a part-time basis. The harassed owners of such concerns will often be very pleased to have a professional secretary calling once a week or so to keep the paperwork under control. Larger organisations may also take you on as an occasional freelance 'temp' – especially as your rates are likely to be considerably less than those charged by temporary staff agencies.

Getting yourself known is the major problem in setting up this kind of service. Mail shots, directed personally to the most likely businesses in your area, together with a series of bold newspaper advertisements, will probably reap the best rewards. But you will need to stick at it. Small businesses which have struggled on for years without clerical staff may not realise what a benefit you could be. Larger organisations, used to dealing with town centre agencies, might be dubious about taking on a freelance temp. Follow up your mail shot with telephone calls: if possible, ask if you can call in personally to discuss your service and how it can enhance/improve the quality (and therefore by implication the profit) of the business concerned.

Providing your own portable word-processing equipment for such a service can be expensive and it would be unrealistic to transport a desktop PC around with you. They are quite heavy and moving them around a lot is very likely to cause damage. Portable 'lap top' computers are currently very popular, with all the major manufacturers now producing at least one model. However, they are still prohibitively expensive for a mobile secretarial service. A better option (and one that prevents you having to lug the printer along too) would be an electric or electronic typewriter.

Bookkeeping

Bookkeeping, either at the client's premises or your own, is a valuable and much demanded skill in its own right. Combine it with a good range of secretarial abilities and you are on to a real winner.

If your bookkeeping skills are rusty (or non-existent), there are classes at colleges of further education which will bring you up to peak form. It is also possible to learn bookkeeping and basic accounting by correspondence course. This is often a very good method of learning the basics because you can take the course at your own pace and in your own time.

Another possibility, and one that is fairly popular, is to join forces with someone who already has good bookkeeping skills but lacks word-processing ability. If you don't want to go into full partnership, it is possible to combine some of your mutual needs (such as advertising a bookkeeping/word-processing service simultaneously and thus reducing the costs of both members), while retaining independence when it comes to actually doing the work and taking the profits. One of you takes the bookkeeping, the other takes the word-processing, and you invoice the customer separately. You can also usefully pass on work to each other: many business users of a word-processing service have occasional bookkeeping needs and vice versa. You will, in addition, have someone to do *your* books, perhaps in return for some word-processing!

Telephone answering

Again, there are a lot of small businesses who could use a telephone answering service: plumbers, electricians, salesmen, decorators, in fact anyone who is usually on the move and therefore not available to take telephone calls. You can charge customers a quarterly fee plus a small additional sum determined by the number of calls received for them. Some telephone answering services charge a flat weekly rate (£5–£15 per week being typical).

A number of companies also advertise for people to provide a telephone answering service. These companies more often than not want you to act as their 'local' agent – either passing on contacts to them or actually dealing with them yourself. They may want to leave samples on your premises; check the implications with your insurance company before agreeing. You may be offered a commission on sales rather than a set fee or weekly rate, so make sure that you know what you're letting yourself in for if you take on something like this.

A well-organised telephone answering service can make a small profit if properly run, but it does have a number of drawbacks. First, you will have to stay in the house for most of the day, every day. This may be ideal if you are virtually housebound anyway but can be quite a strain if you are normally able to get out and about. (You won't even be able to go out to buy more paper unless you can get someone to cover for you while you're gone.) Second, if you have a lot of telephone calls for your clients, you may be losing custom for your word-processing service because your *own* customers can't get through.

In addition, your service may be badly affected if your telephone is out of order for any reason. Unlike faults with your word-processing equipment, getting a telephone line repaired is out of your hands and can take quite some time (although priority is usually given to business lines). One freelance accountant lost a considerable amount of business when his line was out of order during a telephone engineers' strike – he had to wait 10 weeks to have it restored. Perhaps the biggest problem of all is that the phone may never stop ringing! This is fine if you can cope with it but it will interfere considerably with your word-processing output.

Computerised business services

This must be the most obvious 'additional' use of your word-processing equipment. Unless you are using a dedicated word processor, you should be able to buy a wide range of business software programs to use with your existing equipment. This will allow you to offer a comprehensive range of services such as maintenance of staff records, wages preparation, bookkeeping and accounts, cash flow forecasting, stock control, invoicing, and storage of information and records of all kinds.

If you want to offer these services, you will need to have a good understanding of the business service you intend to offer (eg payroll) and will, in addition, need to train yourself to use the particular program you buy. Also, if your service includes storing personal information on individuals on computer files (and this includes names and addresses), you will need to register with the Data Protection Registrar, Springfield House, Water Lane, Wilmslow, Cheshire SK9 5AA (0625 535777 for enquiries).

In addition to *general* business programs, you can get programs that are specifically tailored for certain types of small business, such as hoteliers, video rental shops, estate agents and so on. They may be more expensive but are more closely matched to the requirements of one particular type of business. If you have clients who want you to take over and computerise the administration of their business, they may be prepared to pay for a specific computer program and then pay you a monthly or quarterly fee for operating it. Alternatively, if you are (or become) a whizz with a computer, you can do your own programming, producing software tailor-made to your customers' requirements.

Be very careful if you do decide to take over the affairs of a business in this way. You will need to be especially scrupulous about confidentiality and should ensure that you keep at least two copies of the information relevant to that business in case you damage or accidentally erase one copy.

The best way to find out about computers, what they can do and how they do it, is to go out and try some! If you are totally inexperienced, you could get some hands-on experience by taking one of the many computer courses that are available, or, failing that, ask a knowledgeable friend to let you practise on his computer. The frequent computer shows which are held in most large towns are another source of ideas and information, although these are usually so crowded that you will probably not get a chance to try out the hardware and software very effectively.

One other point you might like to consider is that, as well as providing a service for your customers, business software would be useful for running your *own* service too. You can produce invoices, statements, annual accounts, maintain sales and purchase ledgers and cash books, keep a directory of customers, produce financial forecasts and so on, simply by pressing a few keys.

Electronic communications services

You might also like to consider offering telex, teletex or other electronic mail services to local businesses which lack these facilities. Advances in computer communications technology mean that you can now link up a PC, word processor, or even some electronic typewriters, to the telephone network and use these services at a fraction of the cost of using dedicated equipment (such as the 'old' telex machines).

As well as a computer, you will need a modem. This device converts the signals produced by your computer into a form that can be sent down the telephone line. You will also need a suitable interface to convert parallel signals to series signals (your computer may have one built in), a telephone socket (essential for some modems) and a program that will allow your computer to work as part of a 'network'. The program is normally supplied with the modem. Your local computer supplier will be able to advise you on the requirements of your system. You can obtain a complete package (modem, interface, software and network subscription) for around £100–£200.

Demand for this kind of service is unlikely to be high and you should undertake some market research before launching into electronic communications services. Advances in other kinds of rapid long-distance communication services, particularly facsimile, have taken the steam out of electronic mail to some extent. The main users seem to be large organisations which communicate extensively by computer networks, and home-based enthusiasts. The market for an independent service is dwindling.

Facsimile

Facsimile has really taken off in recent years and many businesses now have a 'fax' machine which is basically a long-range photocopier. Your fax machine scans the original (which might be a printed document, a drawing or a diagram) and sends signals via the public telephone network to a remote destination where the 'copy' is reproduced on the receiver's fax machine. This is useful if you have customers who want to send copies of drawings or diagrams long distances very quickly. Some machines can be used as an ordinary telephone (which obviates the need to have an extra line put in) and have a photocopying facility. The Brother Fax 150, for example, has these features plus the usual facsimile options such as number memory and auto or manual use.

You should be able to obtain a basic fax machine for under £500 and they are continuing to fall in price. You will also need special 'thermal' paper on which to receive facsimiles: this costs from about £4 to £10 per roll depending on make and length.

An additional point in favour of offering a facsimile transmission service is that the recipient doesn't need his own machine to get copies quickly. The Post Office have a special service called Intelpost which allows you to transmit to the Intelpost office nearest the destination address, from where it can be collected or delivered within hours.

The service can be marketed in the same way as a photocopying service and can either stand alone or be offered as part of a more comprehensive business services package. Make sure that your charges cover the cost of the service, which should include use of the machine, time and the cost of the telephone call (and don't forget to allow for the cost of the paper when receiving incoming faxes).

Audio-typing

This is another very lucrative sideline service that you can offer. It is very easy to learn and you can teach yourself how to audio-type once you have the equipment. You will need a very good command of English grammar, spelling and punctuation if you are going to undertake audio-typing, and you may find the lack of 'copy' somewhat distracting. You'll probably find yourself looking at the VDU screen as you type which can cause some touch-typists to stall. Learning to fix your attention elsewhere can help you to overcome this problem.

Unlike copy typing, where you may actively avoid taking an interest in the meaning of the text, while audio-typing you will need to understand the sense of the sentence in order to avoid silly mistakes with similar sounding words, such as bear/bare, forth/fourth, bored/board, formally/formerly and so on. Ask your customers to speak clearly and distinctly, to indicate punctuation and paragraphing throughout the dictation, and to provide a list (in dictation order) of spellings of real names, place names and specialist terms.

Chapter 6 deals with the equipment you will need. Charge extra for the service itself and for providing the use of any dictation machinery and tapes.

Desktop publishing

Desktop publishing (DTP) is a computer application that has rapidly moved from innovation to maturity and is an obvious next stop for an expanding and successful word-processing service. It started out as a package called PageMaker which could be used on Apple Macintosh machines and, because it was such an advance on word-processing, demanded a new name – thus the term 'desktop publishing' was born. More recently, the market has entered a phase of consolidation with DTP and WP packages offering similar facilities.

DTP is exactly what it sounds like: producing material that looks as if it has been professionally typeset, pasted up and printed, using a PC, appropriate software and a 'desktop' (usually laser) printer. A DTP program allows you to manipulate the layout and appearance of text, and to integrate this with graphics, to create an attractive visual impact.

An important feature of DTP programs is the need to operate in conjunction with other software systems. This is because the 'text' is normally typed into a WP program and then 'imported' into the DTP program. Likewise, any graphics (pictures, diagrams etc) you want to use need to be created elsewhere and imported for use in the final documents. Graphics can originate from art packages or from scanned images. A good DTP package will be able to accept text and graphics from a number of sources.

In a nutshell, a DTP program will let you convert imported text into various typefaces (Times, Helvetica, Dutch, Swiss etc) in a range of sizes (points) and styles (eg bold, italic, underlined). You will have a choice of page sizes and the ability to manipulate margins, tabs and page orientation – for example, whether to have the document in 'portrait' or 'landscape'. The ability to arrange text in newspaper columns and flowing round graphics is standard, but most programs allow you to position text in various sized 'blocks' anywhere on the page. You will also be able to position, reduce/enlarge, modify and crop graphics and see the overall effect of your efforts (WYSIWYG) prior to printing.

DESKTOP PUBLISHING

Until recently, DTP programs for PCs were fairly expensive. Well-known packages such as Rank Xerox Ventura Publisher and Aldus PageMaker still retail for £400-£500 but the cheaper, slightly less advanced (and less complicated), programs such as Timeworks DPT and Fleet St Editor currently retail at under £100.

You may need to consider upgrading the memory of your PC in order to use a DTP program effectively. Although the cheaper programs (like Timeworks) *will* work on a basic 512 k machine, the operation will be slow and a lot of disk swapping will be required. You may also experience problems with the printing of complex pages, those with lots of different typefaces, styles, point sizes, columns, graphics and special effects. Both your PC and your printer may need extra memory space to cope with complicated effects. You can purchase 'memory boards' for both PCs and good quality printers which should overcome this problem. Hence, expanding your service to DTP might be a good time at which to consider upgrading your equipment, or at least adding a hard disk to the system which will make life much easier.

Another piece of hardware you may need to acquire is a 'mouse'. This is not a little rodent but a hand-operated pointing device that is tethered to the computer and pushed around on the desktop. The mouse is used to rapidly move the cursor around the screen (called pointing) and to select options by pressing buttons on the mouse (called clicking). Clicking is equivalent to pressing the <ENTER> key. Many DTP packages respond to either the keyboard or a mouse; for others, a mouse may be essential. A mouse is certainly quicker for telling the computer what to do and will cost you between £50 and £120.

One final point to consider is the 'graphics' you are likely to use. Perhaps you will be preparing your own simple graphs and diagrams for inclusion in leaflets, newsletters or brochures. In this case, you may want to consider buying an art package, although this will not transform you into a graphics designer if you have no artistic talent to start with.

An alternative solution is to buy a range of 'graphics' books which have numerous ready-made pictures to choose from. These cost about £30-£50 each. If you want to do this, or if your clients want you to include pictures and diagrams supplied by *them*, you will need a 'scanner'. This is a device, attached to the computer, that is moved over the image to be used and sends signals back to the computer. The screen image produced by the scanner software is a dot-by-dot representation of the actual image and can be subsequently modified if desired. Desktop scanners (flat-bed scanners) are only for the really serious desktop publisher and cost at least £700. Go for a hand-held scanner – these are almost as good if used correctly. You should be able to get one for about £130 (including suitable software). One problem with scanners is that they use a lot of computer memory, so again you may need to upgrade your equipment in order to use one effectively.

With a DTP system, you can offer a wide range of services – the production of newsletters, brochures, advertising leaflets, forms and stationery, manuals, promotional and publicity materials, as well as very high class word-processing. Your charges should reflect the skill, complexity and volume of work required. You will need to be competitive without selling yourself short. Since printing charges vary a lot around the country, it might be a good idea to get a few quotations from local printers to find out what the going rate is in your area.

What kind of clients are likely to need DTP services? The following list indicates some of the assignments my own business was asked to undertake when I first expanded into DTP. As you can see, there are ample opportunities for work!

- Residents' association (newsletters)
- Local training consortium (training materials)
- Pressure groups (leaflets)
- Theatrical groups (publicity materials)
- Garden centre (brochures)
- Hairdressing salon (price lists)
- Various tradesmen (business stationery)
- Video rental shop (case cover design)
- Bus operators (timetables)
- Electrical component manufacturer (manuals)
- Writers' group (booklet)
- Specialist publishers (magazines and journals)
- Consultancy firm (conference programmes and booking forms)
- Local restaurant (menus)
- Students (upmarket dissertations/theses)
- Local authorities (composite timetables)
- Various small businesses (advertising and promotional materials)

Other services

If you are good at something – use it. There is no end to the range of skills that can be usefully combined with word-processing to improve the scope of your service and the income you can derive from it.

Translating
Publishers, large organisations, universities etc frequently require translations of books, reports, technical data and so on. In addition, as Britain's business links with Europe increase in the 1990s, more businesses are going to find themselves in need of translators. The ability to translate the material *and* provide a perfectly printed copy will be invaluable. Write direct to likely organisations offering your service and specifying the language(s) in which you deal. Advertise the facility to local businesses. Rates of pay vary considerably. In general, Chinese and Japanese translators are the best paid, and European language translators the worst.

Teaching
If you can do something, the chances are that you can teach someone else to do it. There are a great many people who are interested in learning how to type, not necessarily to use a typewriter but to improve their keyboard skills to make computer programming easier and quicker. You may also be able to offer courses in word-processing or other computer packages.

A good way to find out what is involved in running courses is to take one yourself, especially if it is some years since *you* learned how to type. You will also need to provide a suitable learning manual and the use of a machine for your students, as well as devising an appropriate course structure and timetable. Try advertising in the local press, in shop windows and on notice boards. You should be able to earn £10–£20 per hour teaching a class of two to eight people.

English and specialist terminologies
Perhaps you are very good at spelling, grammar and punctuation. You could offer to rewrite reports, dissertations, letters and so on for an additional charge. Likewise, if you have a knowledge of any specialist terminologies (medical, legal, scientific etc), you might consider offering your services to doctors, solicitors and other professional people.

Proof-reading
If you are good at spotting typographical errors, you might like to consider offering your services to publishers. Unfortunately, this is a difficult market to get into as those publishers who use

external proof-readers usually have a good supply already and prefer people with extensive publishing experience. You could try writing to several publishers offering your services (you will find a list in the *Writers' and Artists' Yearbook*, published by A and C Black).

You might stand a better chance of getting your name known among publishers if you can do proof-reading for local writers; ask them to recommend you to their publishers. Take advantage of any specialist knowledge or training you may have. If you are conversant with medical terminology, for example, you may stand a better chance of entering the market if you write to publishers who specialise in medical textbooks.

Chapter 9
How to Cope with Your Growing Business

Once your word-processing business is established and you have a good regular supply of work, you may want to consider expanding your service. You can do this very simply and easily from home and it is an excellent stepping stone to opening your own business services bureau.

If you are advertising effectively and providing a good service, you should almost always have an excess of work. There are a number of ways in which you can utilise this excess to increase your profit. The most obvious method is to work longer hours yourself – and this may be your first inclination when more work starts to come in. However, once you are regularly getting more work than you can cope with, you should consider getting help. While you are working from home, you will probably not want to employ someone else. Taking on a subcontractor or forming a partnership may be the answer.

Subcontracting

This is not the same as offering other self-employed WP operators work that you cannot fit in yourself. An agreement with another word-processing business that you will pass on excess work to each other does not usually involve one WP operator working 'for' the other. The advantage of such a system is that the work-load can be distributed between the two businesses and not be lost to another source.

When you subcontract work to another party, *you* remain responsible to the customer for the delivery and quality of the finished product and *you* invoice the customer for payment. The person who actually does the word-processing is paid by you but is not your employee – he is working in a self-employed capacity, just as you are. This sort of agreement can work very well. There are many skilled typists and WP operators with time to spare who wish to make a little money working part time but do not want to become involved in setting up their own business. You may well have family, friends or acquaintances who fall into this category.

Selecting subcontractors

The time when you suddenly find yourself with an excess of work that you cannot, or do not want to, turn away is *not* the time to start looking for a suitable subcontractor. The quality of the work your subcontractor turns out will reflect on *your* service and reputation, not theirs. You will want to spend some time making sure that whoever you choose for subcontracting work is suitably skilled, reliable and can produce work to the required standard in a given time.

Many self-employed WP operators ask friends or relatives to undertake excess word-processing work for them. This can be something of a mixed blessing. Whereas you may know the person concerned very well and be fully aware of his skills, you may also have great difficulty in providing the necessary guidance and criticism in the event of delays, errors or other problems associated with the work produced. One WP operator, during a seasonal flush of dissertations, asked his sister (who worked for a firm of solicitors) to type some of the dissertations in her spare time. He offered a reasonable rate for the work (allowing a small profit for himself) and loaned her a portable word processor. Many of the dissertations were urgent and the WP operator had (on the basis of his sister's assurances) guaranteed that they would be done on time. Unfortunately, his sister found the work much more demanding than she had anticipated and backed out of her agreement after the first dissertation. To make matters worse, the dissertation that *had* been prepared had been very badly done and he had to redo it. He didn't have the heart to complain and paid her the agreed rate for the first dissertation anyway. Although this WP operator *did* manage to get all the dissertations completed on time by working extremely long hours for several weeks, the finished result was far below his usual high standard. The answer is not to offer work to your family or friends unless you are certain that they can do the work satisfactorily in the required time. They also need to appreciate that they are being paid to do work (albeit in a self-employed capacity) and should not be under the impression that they are 'doing you a favour'.

Advertising for subcontractors is sometimes effective. Secretarial students are often happy to take on spare-time work of this kind (try advertising on college/university notice boards). You could also put an advertisement in your local newspaper. It might be wise to use a box number for replies otherwise you may find yourself swamped with telephone calls.

Word the advertisement carefully so that respondents understand that you are *not* offering employment. The money they earn from you will be treated as self-employed earnings and they will be liable for their own tax and National Insurance payments. It is also better – to avoid subcontractor v employee disagreements – if the subcontractors use their own equipment and work on their own premises. You will also want to satisfy yourself about their typing/WP skills, discretion and reliability.

Sort through your replies and select a half-dozen likely applicants. You will not need to conduct the formal sort of interview that would be necessary for employees, but you will want to see candidates personally to discuss both your requirements and their availability. Ask them to complete a simple word-processing test and perhaps a proof-reading test to demonstrate their competence. Once you have decided on one or two potential subcontractors, you should write to the other applicants thanking them for their interest and either declining their offers (if they are obviously unsuitable) or informing them that you will bear them in mind for future subcontracting work.

Using subcontractors

Try to avoid giving a new subcontractor a very long, complicated or important piece of work. Reserve these for yourself. For their first assignment, offer them a task in which the odd mistake will not matter too much and which you yourself can check quickly before passing on to the customer. Initial drafts, envelope addressing and straightforward letters are suitable.

Make sure that your subcontractors are fully aware of your standards and requirements. If necessary, provide samples of the way you want the work laid out and ensure that your subcontractors know *when* you expect them to complete the assignment. You should also stress the need for confidentiality. Your subcontractors should feel the same need to provide a first class, confidential service that you do.

Don't be afraid to delegate to an established and obviously competent subcontractor. Just like employees, good subcontractors will do their best when they have an interest and incentive in the work and when they feel that their abilities are valued.

Paying subcontractors

The rate you agree to pay your subcontractor(s) will obviously be less than you charge your customers. First, make an allowance for any costs you have: eg providing paper, wear and tear on any equipment you provide, any overheads involved, travelling expenses, advertising and so on. Then make an allowance for your time spent (a) with the customer, (b) explaining what is required with the subcontractor and (c) proof-reading the finished assignment (this should only be necessary the first few times you use a subcontractor). After deducting these costs from the estimated charge to the customer, you should also make an allowance for your own profit (say 10 per cent) before deciding how much you can pay the subcontractor for the work. You may need to increase your charges to cover the use of subcontractors if you are still going to make a profit.

Your subcontractors will want to know how much you are going to pay them before they undertake the work, so you will have to make a careful estimate of your own costs, fees and profit margins beforehand. It is probably better to err on the side of underpaying your subcontractors initially. It is much more satisfactory if you find you can increase their rate of payment later on, rather than have to ask them to accept a reduced rate for subsequent work because you have not estimated your costs (of which paying them will be a substantial part) accurately enough.

Don't feel mean because the subcontractor is earning less for doing the work than you would be if you were doing it personally. Your subcontractors are not taking the risks – they are not paying for advertising, paper or the maintenance of equipment. They do not have to deal with customers or keep detailed business records. In addition, they may have a lower requirement for a higher, regular, income. For many subcontractors, word processing is likely to be a part-time 'pin-money' affair. They can take it or leave it, and do not have to suffer the consequences, if the work is badly done or not done at all, that *you* are accepting when you take the work on.

On the other hand, you won't keep good, reliable subcontractors if you pay them a very poor rate while you yourself are making a substantial profit on your charges to the customer, especially if they find out how much *you* were paid – and this is not as difficult as you might think. Make a reasonable profit by all means but don't use your subcontractors as a source of slave labour.

Some contractors can be rather unscrupulous and may try to eliminate you as the 'middle-man' by going directly to your customer and offering to undertake the work for a reduced rate (more than you were paying the subcontractor but less than you were charging the customer). This is, fortunately, a very rare occurrence (partly because the subcontractor can usually only get away with it once!) but it can be rather distressing.

One way to avoid such a situation is to ensure that your subcontractor does not have access to your customers' names and addresses. This can be difficult for some assignments (eg letters, invoices, accounts preparation and so on) where the customer's name appears in the text. It may be better to keep these for yourself. It is also a good idea to avoid giving the subcontractor repeat assignments for *one* particular customer, or a very important customer. In these circumstances, eliminating you could be very tempting to the subcontractor (since there is clearly a lot of work to be had from that customer) and could be financially disastrous for you (if the customer you lose supplied a substantial amount of work for your business).

Going into partnership

Taking on one or more partners is an obvious alternative to subcontracting but needs very careful consideration. The advantages are that your partner will have an equal stake in the word-processing service and will therefore have a greater incentive to work hard, keep deadlines and meet commitments than a subcontractor would. On the other hand, your profit (or earnings) may not increase very much, if at all. After all, your partner will probably expect to take the same profit as you do. Thus, your business may expand in terms of work and cash flow, but your own personal earnings may not increase at all.

Choosing a partner

Some of the factors you should consider when choosing a partner were outlined in Chapter 2. In general, partnerships in which the partners have complementary skills seem to work best. If you are a whizz at word-processing and desktop publishing but find it difficult to deal with customers or handle the organisation of your business, an outgoing and efficient partner who finds it easy to deal with people and administration would be ideal for you. If you're a poor proof-reader, perhaps you could pick a partner who is a good one. If you're a fast WP operator but don't know a thing about other computer applications, a partner who knows about computers (but perhaps can't type) would allow your service to offer a range of computer services in addition to word-processing.

As well as skills and abilities, you should consider the personality and character of your potential partner. You may have known someone personally for years but getting on well socially is no guarantee that you will be able to work together effectively as partners.

Before you form a partnership, sit down with the person(s) concerned and discuss exactly who is going to do what in the business, how profits will be split, how costs will be met and so on. It is relatively easy to decide on general things; problems tend to arise over specific things, such as who is going to work on an assignment that neither partner wants to do, whose name will appear first in advertisements, how will the work-load be split, who will be responsible for making purchases or writing up the books? Will the partners take customers in turn as they come in or will each partner deal exclusively with a particular group of customers, and how will the profits be allocated under such a system? What will happen if one partner feels that he is doing more work, or works faster, than the other? What about the tips and gratuities that satisfied customers frequently bestow on valued WP operators? How will these be divided, if at all? Matters such as these, if left undecided, can cause a great deal of friction.

Legal aspects

Apart from the practical aspects of actually getting along with your partner(s), you should also consider your legal position. However small your word-processing service, it would be prudent to have a formal partnership agreement drawn up by a solicitor. I have known of several 'partnerships' that regretted not doing this. One small word-processing/desktop publishing business started as an informal partnership between three young ladies who each contributed £500 'capital' and provided their own equipment. One of the partners, a graphic designer, produced a 'logo' for the business which was printed on stationery, brochures, advertising materials and so on. The business made a loss for the first three months and the graphics designer decided to leave the partnership. The others agreed that she should be allowed to take her £500 investment and equipment (even though she should really have sustained part of the losses) and carried on without her. Three months later, the business really took off. The partner who had left was rather annoyed and decided that the 'logo' she had designed belonged exclusively to her and not to the business. She took the remaining two partners to court in order to prevent them from using it. A long legal battle ensued during which the original business, which was showing real promise, became bankrupt. If they had had a formal partnership agreement, these problems would have been relatively easily solved.

Basically, a partnership agreement defines the relationship between the partners and with third parties, and will protect the partners in the event of any dispute or breakdown in the relationship. The Small Firms Service in its leaflet 'Starting and Running Your Own Business' recommends that a partnership agreement should include the following minimum details:

- Name and nature of business and commencing date.
- The amount of capital to be provided by each partner.
- The role of each partner clearly defined.
- The apportioning of profits and losses.
- Voting rights, how will decisions be made? Will one partner have overall control or will each have equal voting rights?
- The duration of the partnership.
- Arrangements for dissolving the partnership or releasing a partner.
- Provision for admitting new partners or getting rid of an existing partner.
- Arrangements for arbitration if the partners disagree.
- Arrangements concerning the retirement or death of a partner.
- How the bank account is to be operated.
- The preparation and auditing of annual accounts.
- What provision is to be made in the event of prolonged absence of a partner through sickness or accident.
- Insurance against death or sickness of a partner and for the business generally.
- Provision for holidays and other time off.
- Provision and use of cars.

Another important point, noted in Chapter 2 but well worth repeating here, is that partners are held responsible for each other's debts in relation to the word-processing business. Thus, if your partner makes a rash purchase or buys a lot of goods on credit and then disappears, *you* will be responsible for those debts. This also applies to income tax liability. If your partner fails to pay his share of income tax, the Inland Revenue can ask *you* to pay it.

Chapter 10
Starting an Office Services Bureau

Running a word-processing service from home requires the minimum of capital investment, offers considerable flexibility in terms of working hours and the type of work taken on, and can be run entirely single-handed on a very low budget. Once you decide to open an office services bureau, you will need to reassess your own skills, abilities and commitments, the financial outlay required and the potential market (which will be somewhat different to that of a home-based service), and prepare an entirely new financial forecast for the business.

Bringing in the professionals

Your home-based service was probably such a low risk affair that you didn't feel it necessary to consult the usual expert sources before embarking on it. Although a town centre bureau should have as much chance of success as a home-based service, the financial and legal implications require you to take a much longer and more serious look at your chances of success before you embark on the project. If your home-based word-processing service had been a disaster, you would have lost very little; if your office-based service fails, you stand to lose much more, especially if you have a large loan or overdraft and have purchased a lot of expensive equipment.

This is the time to bring in the professionals. But remember, they can only offer you advice and information; they cannot guarantee your success. Take advice by all means but make the decisions yourself. It's *your* business: *you* must decide how it is run.

Bank managers

This is probably the first person you will wish to consult. Your own personal bank, or the one you have been using for your business account so far, is probably the best one to use. As well as the usual financial advice, and the ability to arrange loans or overdrafts as necessary, your bank manager may be able to offer you advice on many commercial and business matters. He should have a good knowledge of local affairs and other business establishments.

If you require a loan or overdraft to purchase equipment for the bureau, your bank manager will want to see a detailed financial forecast (along the lines outlined in Chapter 2) for the new business. Take along the accounts for your current home-based service as well. These will demonstrate your entrepreneurial ability and the accuracy of your previous financial forecasts, and indicate the success you have already achieved in a business of this kind. All the major banks have kits which show you how to produce a suitable business plan and it may be a good idea to ask for one of these in advance, so that you are fully prepared before you approach the manager.

The government's loan guarantee scheme guarantees loans by banks and financial institutions to firms unable to obtain conventional loans because they lack security or a track record. The government guarantees 70 per cent (85 in certain inner city areas) of loans over two to seven years in return for a premium of 2.5 per cent on the guaranteed portion. Ask your bank about this facility if you have any difficulty financing your expansion.

Consultations with and advice provided by bank managers are usually free.

Accountants

In addition to preparing and auditing accounts, a good accountant can provide advice on a number of other matters related to the financial side of your proposed office services bureau, such as buying or leasing premises, keeping your tax liability to a minimum, dealing with VAT, employing staff and so on.

Although having an accountant to prepare your annual accounts is not a statutory requirement for sole traders and partnerships, you may wish to consider engaging one once your business expands. The principles will be the same but the accounts will probably be rather more complicated because additional factors such as staff, premises, creditors and debtors will have to be taken into account. An accountant will also help you to prepare a financial forecast for presentation to your bank and can provide management accounts which will help you to see how the business is going and how it could be improved.

Consultations with an accountant can be expensive. A freelance accountant will normally charge less than a large firm. Ask about fees before the consultation and don't forget to get an invoice and receipt so that you can charge it to your business.

Solicitors

The volume of legislation concerning industry and commerce is far too wide in scope and complex in detail for the busy owner of an office services bureau to have time to understand it all. Solicitors tend to specialise so it makes sense to use one knowledgeable in commercial and employment law. Most family solicitors are *not* normally involved in these aspects; however, your personal solicitor may be able to put you in touch with another who does specialise in this field. A firm of commercial solicitors with partners who are specialists in different branches of the law is ideal.

You may never need a solicitor but it is sensible to engage one to cover any legal problems should they arise (eg chasing up bad debts). You can have a free initial consultation with a solicitor offering general business information through the Lawyers for Enterprise Scheme. Telephone 071-405 9075 for details.

As with accountants, the services of a good commercial law solicitor can be expensive, but lack of specialist advice and backing could lead to heavy losses.

Insurance brokers

As mentioned in Chapter 3, insurance is such a complicated business that you would be well advised to consult an insurance broker at the outset. He will be able to tell you which insurances are necessary and which are desirable for your particular office services bureau, and should be able to get you the best 'deal' for your requirements.

The services of an insurance broker are free and his advice should be impartial. (Brokers also carry professional indemnity insurance which means you can sue them if their advice is so bad that you lose money as a result.)

The broker should get two or three quotations from different insurance companies for you. Before you accept any proposals, ask your accountant for advice on the tax aspects of the insurance.

If you have been running a word-processing service from home for some time, you will probably already have insurance cover for your equipment and to cover customers and any employees. This will need to be revised when you start an office services bureau. There are many types of insurance for businesses. Employer's liability insurance is required by law. Others of possible interest include public liability, fidelity guarantee (covering fraud by employees), fire, theft, personal accident, sickness, legal costs, health and pensions. 'Packaged' insurances are available for small businesses in which one policy covers your premises, equipment, personal insurance, employer's and public liability and so on at less cost than individual policies. Ask your broker about these.

Free professional help and advice

Chapter 3 gives details of the wealth of free advice and information available to new and existing small businesses. If you do not feel the need to seek advice from these sources when you started your home-based business, you will certainly want to do so now. In addition, the Small Firms Service has a specialist counselling service for established businesses thinking about expansion called the Business Development Service.

Buying an existing bureau

You may want to consider buying an existing office services bureau. There are advantages in this. First, you will save time and effort in decorating and equipping your own establishment. You should also have a ready-made supply of customers used to trading with the previous owner. You will eliminate the 'dead' period during which you are too busy to continue your home-based service but haven't yet set up or attracted sufficient custom to your office-based service. The owner may also be prepared to offer you advice based on his experience in the business. Finally, buying an existing bureau may work out cheaper than renting or buying an office which has to be converted, decorated and equipped from scratch.

The benefits may be offset by disadvantages however. The owner may have had a bad reputation with customers and/or creditors which you will have to overcome before you can make the service successful. The location may be poor or the service lacking sufficient custom. Ask yourself why the owner wants to sell the business – does the reason sound genuine? Does he intend to set up another word-processing service in the town? The fixtures, fittings and equipment may be outdated or in bad condition. You may not want to adopt someone else's business – especially if your own home-based service has been a great success and you have established customers of your own – although it is possible to change the name of the business and announce the new ownership.

Examine the equipment carefully, determine its age and obtain evalutions of similar machines. Find out if parts and service agreements are still available. Check whether the equipment has been fully paid for and whether the business has any outstanding debts. Will the owner leave the present telephone number and the name of the business or will these need to be changed? Are the premises owned or leased? How long does the lease run and who actually owns the premises? Ask to see copies of all the relevant documents – lease, receipts for equipment, service/maintenance contracts, guarantees and so on – as well as the business's annual accounts. Check whether the local authority has any future development plans for the area; these may have a dramatic effect (positive or negative) on your service.

If you do decide to buy an existing bureau, have the sales agreement draw up by a solicitor. It should include a description of what is being sold, the purchase price, the method of payment, the buyer's assumption of transferable maintenance agreements and guarantees, and a covenant with the seller not to compete within a certain period of time. If the service is still in operation, then the agreement should also include the date and procedures of closing/re-opening under the new ownership.

If you buy an existing office services bureau, you will probably be asked to pay something for the 'goodwill'. This represents the value of business which may come to you as a result of the previous owner's efforts: satisfied customers, advertising and promotion etc. Discuss this with your professional adviser and check whether existing customers are likely to keep coming to you before the sum, if any, is agreed.

Above all, if you are thinking about buying an existing word-processing bureau, seek the advice of your solicitor or accountant. The legal process of handing over the business in exchange for cash or a loan should in any case be handled by a solicitor. Taking professional advice may involve a small expense but *not* taking it can be very costly indeed.

Starting afresh

If you don't want to buy an existing business (or there isn't one for sale in your area), you will need to buy or rent suitable premises and start up your own office from scratch. Buying premises is not a good idea at the start as it ties up your capital and selling could be difficult and time-consuming should you need to dispose of the property quickly. On the other hand, property does tend to increase in value and is likely to be a good investment from that point of view. Premises are also useful collateral against which to borrow money in the future and you will not be faced with unpredictable increases in lease rental at inconvenient times.

Leasing is by far the most usual way of acquiring business premises. Commercial leases run for relatively short periods: usually between three and seven years, with rent reviews at the end of each term or sooner. This adds an unknown factor to the long-term future of an office services bureau in rented premises. If your business is successful, you don't want to have to move into new premises at the end of three years because the rent increase is too high. You will need to look at the advantages and disadvantages of both before deciding on the best option for you. Further information can be found in *How to Choose Business Premises* by H Green, B Chalkley and P Foley (Kogan Page).

Finding premises
There are several options open to you when you are looking for premises. Newspapers are a good place to start. Commercial and business properties are advertised in publications such as *Dalton's Weekly*. Local newspapers usually carry advertisements for business premises in the region. Many local authorities now provide offices and workshops for small businesses or new ventures – occasionally with rent-free periods. Estate agents often have a commercial and business department which specialises in rented premises; local enterprise agencies are also a good source of information about locally available premises.

Location and suitability of premises
You will probably want to locate in the business or commercial centre of your town. When considering location, several points should be borne in mind. Will your business be visible from the street? (This can have important consequences for the number of customers you can attract.) How easy is it for customers to reach the office? What, if any, competition will you have in the immediate area?

You will also want to consider the number and size of rooms available, the state of decoration and repair, the toilet/washroom/kitchen facilities and requirements to comply with fire safety regulations (which may affect any internal alterations you have in mind). The security of the premises should also come high on your list. You will have quite a lot of expensive computing, printing and office equipment on the premises which you will need to protect from theft. Are there locks on accessible windows? Is there an alarm system? Can the doors be secured properly (with mortice locks)? Who else has access to the building: how are shared entrances/facilities protected?

Other factors worth considering are the state of the electrical supply and the level of humidity in the premises. In a relatively modern, purpose-built, office complex, you should have no problems with either the electricity supply or damp air – both of which can play havoc with word-processing equipment! If the premises are close to workshops and/or share an electricity supply, you may find that surges can occur which can seriously affect your computer equipment. This can be overcome by buying special adaptors from electrical/computer supplies which prevent electrical surges from reaching your equipment. It is probably a good idea to have these fitted as a matter of course since the operation of your own equipment can cause fluctuations in the supply. Certain locations may also be more prone to excessive heat or damp than others. Would your equipment have to be positioned in front of windows? How hot would your computers get on a sunny day? Would it be possible to open windows for ventilation without admitting damp air (eg from a restaurant kitchen)?

As well as the length and cost of any lease, you will need to consider the amount required for internal decoration and fittings and external sign painting. Check whether the lessor is prepared to make a contribution towards any redecoration, repair or alteration required.

Think about the amount of space you are going to need. How many desks will you have? How much space do you need to provide for photocopiers, display stands, printers, word processors and seating for customers? How will the space be divided up? You may need planning permission if starting your office services bureau will entail a change of use of the premises you have selected. Be sure to check what the existing planning use is. If in doubt, consult either your solicitor or the planning office of your local authority.

Once you have one or two suitable premises in mind, it can be a good idea to make a diagram (on squared paper) of the internal layout. Cut out proportionally sized shapes corresponding to the fittings and equipment you have in mind and see how these would fit. You will also want to consider the number and positions of sockets and lighting points (an office services bureau will need a lot of these).

Will you have a separate room for discussions with customers or will you conduct all your business in a large open office? Do you want premises with a small office frontage and reception desk where customers can be dealt with, while keeping the main bulk of the equipment and work area out of sight? Visit some other office services bureaux. How are their offices laid out?

Which ones appear to offer the most attractive and professional service?

Furnishing and decor

Once you have selected your premises, you will need to think about furnishing and decor. While it would be wasteful to spend vast sums creating your ideal office environment, it would be equally rash to start your office services bureau in tatty, poorly furnished surroundings. The image you create, especially in the reception area, will influence both potential and existing customers. Your offices should be clean, airy and uncluttered. It may be worth investing in new carpeting and perhaps having the walls and ceilings emulsioned. Perhaps you could offer to do some word-processing or printing in return for decorating services?

Again, it is not strictly necessary to buy new desks for yourself and your staff. Good quality second-hand desks should look good and will last longer than brand new but inferior ones. Spend more on the reception area and display stands and on ensuring that any window display area is well decorated and attractive. You might like to consider including plants and comfortable chairs, especially if customers have to wait for service or photocopies. You can now buy large tubs of imitation plants which look very realistic but need no maintenance (apart from the odd wash). They cost about as much as the real thing but tend to survive an office environment rather better!

Keep looking good

There is little point in decorating your offices and providing attractive lighting, seating and displays if you then let it become run-down, dirty or untidy. Make sure that any areas where customers have access, or can see, are kept clean and free from disorganised piles of paper. Make arrangements to have any windows cleaned once a fortnight or so, and either clean the interior of the offices yourself or hire a cleaner to do the job for you once or twice a week. Office complexes that house several small businesses often 'share' the services of a cleaner. Make sure that your staff understand that papers, rubbish, cups of tea and take-away meals are not to be taken to, or left in, the reception area.

Stock and equipment

Your equipment needs will be dictated by the size and range of services you are initially going to offer. You will certainly need a minimum of two PCs or dedicated WPs, two desks, a filing cabinet, a reception desk (higher than a conventional desk because it is intended to be *stood* at), a photocopier, typists' and customers' chairs, and storage cupboards.

You may also need to reconsider your stock suppliers. While you were working from home, and certainly while you were working single-handed, your stock turnover will have been relatively slow and you may have been quite content to get everything from local suppliers. Your town centre office services bureau will have a much higher stock turnover and you will therefore need to investigate bulk suppliers. You may find that you can have bulk supplies delivered to your premises much more cheaply by large wholesalers than by the small stationers you have been dealing with. Time spent researching suppliers and costs will be invaluable later on. While you are enquiring, ask about discounts, credit facilities and advertising displays.

Costing, pricing and estimating

You will need to completely reassess your costs following the same basic rules you used for your home-based service (see Chapter 4). Your basic costs will be very much higher once you start operating from office premises. Rent, rates, wages, maintenance of premises, higher insurance premiums, fees for professional services, loan repayments and so on will all increase your cost-per-job rate. This means that you will have to start charging your customers a higher rate. You may also need (or want) to start charging VAT.

As a town centre bureau, you will have many more customers than a home-based word-processing service, and the fact that you will probably be offering a wider range of services means that your new venture should be as successful as, or even more so than, your old one. Ironically, you will probably find that most customers are prepared to pay more, wait longer for completion and be rather less 'finicky' about minor errors and corrections than they would be when dealing with a home-based WP operator. Don't let this make you complacent. You are in the big league now and will need to keep on your toes if you are not going to let your competitors attract the majority of the market.

Chapter 11
Taking on Staff

Once your word-processing business has progressed beyond the one-person operation stage, you will have to deal with the selection, motivation and training of staff. As well as your legal responsibilities, you will have to tackle all aspects of working relations including discipline, dismissal, health and safety, wages negotiations, hours of work and leave. A useful booklet on the subject entitled 'Employing People: The ACAS Handbook for Small Firms' is available from the Small Firms Service or ACAS (see Chapter 12).

Before you advertise for staff, you will need to consider carefully what kind of skills your employees will need, how many hours you need them to work and what (and how) you can pay them. Write a job description for each employee. This will help you to clarify what skills your employees will need, will be useful during interviews when you can specify exactly what will be required, and will help you to formulate your advertisements.

Selecting staff

In a small business where commitment is so important, good working relations crucial and the margin for error small, finding the right staff is vital. There are several ways to find suitable candidates.

One possibility is to take someone on through the Employment Training programme. This will be an unemployed person who wishes to train, or re-train, in a new field. You will be expected to undertake the training of the person involved (and will be offered a choice of two to three candidates) but you can stipulate any essential previous training requirements (eg the ability to type). The benefits to you include the following:

(a) Low cost: you will be expected to make a financial contribution but this will cost less than employing someone.
(b) The opportunity to train someone to do the job *before* you take them on.

(c) The chance to get to know the trainee prior to undertaking a long-term commitment.

You are not obliged to employ the trainee at the end of the (one year) employment training programme. There are two disadvantages. First, the trainee must be allowed to attend a training centre one day a week – this may pose problems if you need someone in the office full time. Also, you have to input time and energy training someone rather than employing a qualified and experienced person from the start. Contact your local Training Agency for further details.

You may already know someone who would be suitable: perhaps someone who has subcontracted for you in the past would be interested. Alternatively, you can advertise in shop windows or local newspapers. Private employment agencies are another possibility, although they may charge a fee (often a percentage of your employee's starting salary) for finding a suitable applicant. Your local Jobcentre will advertise your vacancies and notify you if any suitable people register. Unfortunately, Jobcentres don't tend to be very selective when referring staff to you.

It will help if you can give the Jobcentre full details of the work involved, wages, qualifications needed, training offered and so on. Similarly, the more information you can put in your advertisements the better potential applicants will be able to assess their suitability for the job, and the job's suitability for them.

In the present economic climate, you will probably receive a large number of applications – even for a part-time job that is not exceptionally well paid – so you will need to have a method of sifting through these to select the most appropriate candidates for interview. Don't automatically plump for the highest qualified applicants or those who are prepared to work for the lowest wages: they may simply use you as a stepping stone to more lucrative employment. You want employees who are dedicated, adaptable and versatile. You are most likely to get these if you provide the right incentives (not just money) and if you show your willingness to help them to develop their potential in the job.

An application form (which you can devise and photocopy or print yourself) has the advantage of standardising the information collected from applicants, ensuring that each applicant covers all the questions you want answered. On the other hand, if you ask applicants to apply in writing you may get a better idea of their ability in English, writing, composition and so on.

In any event, you should make notes of any questions you want answered during interview (from gaps in the application form or written application). Preferably, after selecting two or three possibles from the first interview, hold a second interview. Finding the right staff is critical for a small office services bureau so it is as well to take plenty of time over the selection.

You may want to include a typing/word-processing and shorthand/audio-test during the first interview, when you will also be looking, among other things, for punctuality, a neat appearance, confidence and an outgoing, helpful personality. If the applicant is likely to be left in charge of the bureau at any time, you will need to be sure that he/she has the maturity and ability to handle any eventuality. Does the applicant have the appropriate abilities and qualifications? Can he/she deal with customers personally and on the telephone? Does he/she understand the degree of commitment and flexibility that is required in working for a small business?

Once you have made the selection, you will want to offer the job immediately. Do this by telephone and confirm in writing. Ask the prospective employee to accept the offer in writing within a certain time. Be sure to take up references before you offer the job, or make the receipt of satisfactory references a condition of the appointment. In the offer, restate the basic terms of the employment (date of commencement, hours, salary, holidays etc).

You will also need to reject unsuccessful candidates. Write a simple, polite, rejection letter after you have a firm acceptance: *don't* go into the details of why they were unsuccessful.

Discrimination

No matter how small your business, you are not allowed to discriminate against candidates on the grounds of race or sex, or because they are married or have children. It is always a good idea to take full notes during interviews so that you can show, if necessary, your reasons for selecting one candidate in preference to another.

Contracts of employment

As soon as someone starts working for you, you have a legal contract with that person, whether or not anything is written down. Your advertisement, job description and anything you say during interview can be held to be part of that contract, so don't make rash statements. Within 13 weeks of commencement of employment, you must provide the employee(s) with a written statement of the main terms and conditions of employment. This will include your name, the date continuous employment began, pay, hours of work, details of holidays, sick pay and pensions, period of notice, job title, disciplinary rules and grievance procedure. You do not have to provide a written statement to employees who normally work less than 16 hours per week (unless they have worked for you for more than eight hours per week for over five years).

Pay, tax and National Insurance

When deciding how much to pay your employees, you will need to take into account how much you can afford, and think the work is worth to you, and the going rate for similar jobs in your area.

You must inform the tax office that already deals with your business when you take on staff or they leave. They will tell you where your Pay As You Earn (PAYE) tax office will be and that office will send you all the relevant information. You will have to deduct tax from your employees' pay (under the PAYE system) and will be responsible for paying both employer's and employees' Class 1 National Insurance contributions (you deduct the employees' contribution from their pay). Leaflet P7 'Employers Guide to PAYE', available from the Inland Revenue, and leaflet NP15 'Employers Guide to National Insurance Contributions' from the DSS lay down the guide-lines for these deductions. Another source of useful advice is *PAYE: A Working Guide for the Small Business* by C Anderson (Kogan Page); however, your PAYE tax office will send you a comprehensive, and relatively easy to follow, starter pack containing all the instructions and forms you need to operate a simple PAYE system.

You must also provide each employee with a pay slip showing gross pay, itemising deductions, and giving the net sum to be received, on each pay day. Tear-off blocks of pay slips can be purchased from most stationers.

Hours of work, holidays and leave of absence

When deciding which hours, and how many per week, your employee(s) will be needed, you should consider when your peak daily work-loads occur, what provision you need to make for lunch breaks, whether you will be open Saturday and if you will have an early closing day. If you plan to start off with just yourself and one employee, you could consider taking on two part-timers rather than one full-time employee. This gives you greater flexibility and means you won't be left completely single-handed in the event of holidays or sick leave.

Provisions for time off for attending ante-natal clinics, public duties, trade union activities and maternity and sick leave are covered in the leaflet 'Employing People – The ACAS Handbook for Small Firms' obtainable free from the Small Firms Service.

You may need to make some provision for taking on temporary staff during employees' holidays and sick leave. 'Temps' are available from temporary staffing agencies but the fees are usually very high. A good alternative is to take on students (out of term time) or to advertise for suitably qualified temporary staff either in your local paper or through the Jobcentre.

Good working relations

You will get the best results from your employee(s) if you treat them as valuable members of your team rather than simple automatons expected to do little more than follow orders efficiently.

Get into the habit of delegating work: don't try to do everything yourself. Set high standards and provide adequate training and opportunities so that your staff can reach them. Ask for your employees' counsel and help: give them a chance to take part in decisions and try to let them carry out their own ideas. If criticism is necessary, do it constructively. Suggest ways in which their work (or behaviour) could be improved rather than complaining about their faults.

Discipline and dismissal

If you discover a problem, the first thing to do is to investigate it fully. Then tell your employee what the complaint is and give him a chance to explain his side of the problem. The formal procedure demands that you give the employee a verbal warning (confirm this in writing), followed by a final written warning before dismissal can take place, except for gross misconduct. You cannot fire someone if they are carrying out the requirements of the contract you have with them, and beware of giving an inappropriate disciplinary warning.

One secretarial bureau had an employee who worked very well but was persistently late. The manageress eventually warned the employee that if she was not on time for the next 30 days she would be sacked. The employee was punctual for 30 days and then, on the thirty-first day, was late again. She was sacked but went to a tribunal and won. It was a case of unfair dismissal because it was what was known as a 'resolutive warning'. What the manageress should have said was: 'You will be fired it you are late during the next 30 days and thereafter you will be expected to obey the standards demanded by the firm's rules.'

Employment legislation

Although the bulk of employment legislation is there to protect the employee, special provisions have been made in many cases (unfair dismissal, maternity leave and so on) for small businesses. They are excluded from the necessity to comply with certain regulations.

In addition to the basic guide 'Employing People – The ACAS Handbook for Small Firms', a number of pamphlets are available free from the Department of Employment and ACAS providing more detailed information about employment legislation. ACAS also operate an advice service for employers.

Health and safety

Office environments can seem relatively safe but there are hazards involved, especially in the operation of electrical equipment and machinery. Don't have electrical leads trailing over the floor or piles of paper standing around for months. Make sure that potentially dangerous equipment (guillotines, paper shredders, electric staplers etc) have proper guards and that staff are instructed in safety procedures. Make sure that you have adequate insurance cover for staff, customers, premises and property in the event of an accident.

The health and safety regulations are very extensive. Your local office of the Health and Safety Executive will tell you what your legal responsibilities are and a number of free guide-line publications are available. Your local Fire Prevention Officers will advise you about the necessary fire precautions. Another useful source of advice and information is the Royal Society for the Prevention of Accidents, Cannon House, The Priory Queensway, Birmingham B4 6BS (021-200 2461).

Chapter 12
Useful Addresses

Advisory, Conciliation and Arbitration Service (ACAS)
27 Wilton Street, London SW1X 7AZ; 071-210 3000
Also regional offices: consult your local telephone directory
Association of British Chambers of Commerce
Sovereign House, 212a Shaftesbury Avenue, London WC2H 2EW; 071-240 5831
BBC External Services
PO Box 76, Bush House, Strand, London WC2B 4PH; 071-240 3456 (translation/interpretation work)
British Insurance & Investment Brokers Association
BIIBA House, 14 Bevis Marks, London EC3A 7NT; 071-623 9043
Business in the Community
277a City Road, London EC1V 1LX; 071-253 3716/3000
Companies Registration Office
Companies House, Crown Way, Maindy, Cardiff CF4 3UZ; 0222 388588
and
102 George Street, Edinburgh EH2 3DJ; 031-225 5774
and
Chichester House, 43–47 Chichester Court, Belfast BT1 4PJ; 0232 234121
Institute of Scientific and Technical Communicators Ltd
17 Bluebridge Avenue, Brookmans Park, Hatfield, Hertfordshire AL9 7RY; 0707 55392
Law Society
Legal Aid Department, 113 Chancery Lane, London WC2A 1PL; 071-242 1222
Local Enterprise Development Unit
LEDU House, Upper Galwally, Belfast BT8 4TB; 0232 491031

National Federation of Self-employed and Small Businesses Ltd
32 St Anne's Road West, Lytham St Annes, Lancashire FY8 1NY; 0253 720911
and
140 Lower Marsh, London SE1 7AE; 071-928 9272

The Prince's Youth Business Trust
First Floor, 5 The Pavement, Clapham, London SW4 0HY; 071-262 1340
(funding for young people starting their own business)

Scottish Business in the Community (SCOTBIC)
Romano House, 43 Station Road, Edinburgh EH12 7AF; 031-334 9876

Scottish Development Agency
120 Bothwell Street, Glasgow G2 7JP; 041-248 2700

Small Firms Service
This service is gradually being taken over by 82 local Training and Enterprise Councils (TECs). Until the process is complete, use 0800 222999 (Freefone Enterprise) for all offices.

Society of Indexers
Secretary: Mrs H C Troughton, 16 Green Road, Birchington, Kent CT7 9JZ; 0843 41115

The Training Agency
Head Office, Moorfoot, Sheffield S1 4PQ; 0742 753275

Translators' Association
Society of Authors, 84 Drayton Gardens, London SW10 9SD; 071-373 6642

Welsh Development Agency
Pearl House, Greyfriars Road, Cardiff CF1 3XX; 0222 222666

Chapter 13
Further Reading

Starting and running a business

Be Your Own Boss: How to Become Self-employed, John Blundell (National Federation of the Self-employed)
The Business Plan Workbook, C Barrow and P Barrow (Kogan Page)
Croner's Reference Book for the Self-employed and Smaller Business, Croner Publications Ltd, Croner House, London Road, Kingston upon Thames, Surrey KT2 6SR (on annual subscription)
Debt Collection Made Easy, Peter Buckland (Kogan Page)
Everything You Need to Know About Marketing, P Forsyth (Kogan Page)
Financial Management for the Small Business, 2nd edition, C Barrow (Kogan Page)
Forming a Limited Company, P Clayton (Kogan Page)
The Guardian Guide to Running a Small Business, 7th edition, Ed Clive Woodcock (Kogan Page)
How to Choose Business Premises, H Green, B Chalkley and P Foley (Kogan Page)
How to Choose Microcomputers and Software for Your Business, P Beck (Kogan Page)
Law for the Small Business, 7th edition, P Clayton (Kogan Page)
Partnership, I Stratton and I Blackshaw (Oyez)
PAYE: A Working Guide for the Small Business, 2nd edition, C Anderson (Kogan Page)
Running Your Own Business, R Edwards (Oyez)
Successful Marketing for the Small Business, 2nd edition, Dave Patten (Kogan Page)
What's Your Problem? Available from the Action Resource Centre, Belfast Enterprise Centre, ARC House, 103-107 York Street, Belfast BT15 1AB
Working for Yourself: The Daily Telegraph Guide to Self-employment, 14th edition, Godfrey Golzen (Kogan Page)
VAT and the Small Business, E Tirbutt (Kogan Page)

Recommended reference works

A good dictionary, such as *The Concise Oxford Dictionary*, is essential (even if your word-processor has a spell-checker!).

A Dictionary of Modern English Usage, H W Fowler: useful for any problem relating to English grammar or usage.

Roget's Thesaurus of English words and phrases, Penguin. This lists words according to their meaning and is invaluable in helping you to choose the right one. Useful even if your word processor offers a thesaurus.

Whitaker's Almanack, an annual publication, containing factual information.

Chambers Typing and Wordprocessing Dictionary, Stananought and Stananought (Chambers)

Word Processing Dictionary (McGraw-Hill) and *The Information Technology Dictionary* (McGraw-Hill): useful for those new to word-processing.

For those involved in medical work

Dorland's Pocket Medical Dictionary and/or *Baillière's Nurses' Dictionary*

The Medical Secretary's and Receptionist's Handbook, Michael Drury (Baillière Tindall)

Medical Shorthand Dictation Passages, Irene Burgess (Cassell): for New Era shorthand practice.

Medical Words and Phrases, Janice Kerr (Pitman): for Pitman 2000 shorthand practice and reference.

MIMS Published monthly and sent to every GP, this contains a list of all proprietary drugs and will be invaluable when checking the spelling of some of these difficult names.

For those involved in legal work

The Legal Secretary's Handbook, A Newington and H M Willoughby (Oyez Longman)

A Secretary's Guide to the Legal Office, Annette Parry (Pitman): particularly for New Era and 2000 shorthand practice and reference.

For those involved in work for publication

Hart's Rules for Compositors and Readers (Oxford University Press)

The Oxford Dictionary for Writers and Editors (Oxford University Press)

Indexes and Indexing, R L Collison (Ernest Benn)

Typesetting for Micro Users: A Beginner's Guide to Improved Text Presentation (Quorum Technical Services)

Books and magazines on secretarial/office skills

Learning to type
Basic Typing Skills, K Dulmage (Pitman)
Compose and Type, M Tombs (Pitman)
Guide to Wordprocessing & Typing for Beginners, K Fraser and J Collyer (Usborne)
Typing Simplified: A Self Tutored Course, Robinson (McGraw-Hill)
Typing: Two-in-One Course, 2nd edition, A Drummond and A Coles-Mogford (McGraw-Hill): for beginners.

Audio-typing
Audio Transcription, A Drummond (McGraw-Hill)
Elementary Audio-Typing, 2nd edition, Barbara Colley (McGraw-Hill): really designed for teachers of audio-typing, this little A5 book is also useful for self-taught beginners.

Word-processing
15 Hour Wordprocessing: Using the Amstrad WP, A Ruthven (National Extension College): for owners of the Amstrad PCW8256 or PCW8512.
Hands-on WordPerfect, J A Morison (McGraw-Hill): good introductory text for those with no previous experience of WordPerfect.
IBM PC Wordprocessing: WordPerfect, Wordstar, Displaywrite, Multimate, Layman and Renner (Prentice Hall): expensive book explaining how to use some of the more well-known WP programs.
Making the Most of Word Processing, T H Chambers (Business Books)
Text Processing, Joyce and Derek Stananought (Pitman): covers elementary, intermediate and advanced levels of both typewriting and word-processing. Designed for any typewriter or word-processing equipment.
Wordprocessing on Microcomputers, Muehlman (Prentice Hall)

Desk-top publishing
DTP on a Shoestring: With Fleet St Editor, Ian R Sinclair (BSP Professional): good introduction to the use of Fleet St Editor.
DTP on Your PC: Timeworks Publisher Companion, Morrissey

(Sigma Press): comprehensive no-nonsense introduction to DTP using this package.

There are also innumerable guides and handbooks for the more expensive programs *Aldus Pagemaker* and *Venura Publisher*.

DTP with the Amstrad PCW, M Milan (NCC Publications)

Introduction to Desk Top Publishing, D Hewson (J Taylor Book Ventures)

Introduction to Desk Top Publishing, Hulme (South Western Publishing Co)

Free leaflets and guides

The following is a sample of the guides most relevant to a word-processing service.

County Courts
Enforcing Money Judgements in the County Court
Small Claims in the County Court

Small Firms Service
Accounting for a Small Firm
Employing People – The ACAS Handbook for Small Firms
A Guide to Services for Small Businesses
Marketing
The Single Market 1992 – For You. An Action Guide for Smaller Firms
Trade Credit
Your Guide to Government Help for Small Firms
Working for Yourself – What You Need to Know

Rural Development Commission
Action for Rural Enterprise

Department of Social Security
Leaflet CF11 *Application to pay Self-Employed NI Contributions*
Leaflet NI27A *People with Small Earnings from Self-employment*
Leaflet NI41 *National Insurance Guidance for Self-employed People*
Leaflet NI208 *National Insurance Contribution Rates*
Leaflet NP15 *Employers Guide to National Insurance Contributions*

Leaflet NP18 *Class 4 Contributions*
Leaflet NP32 *Your Retirement Pension*

Inspector of Taxes
Leaflet CA1 *Capital Allowances on Machinery or Plant*
Leaflet CGT11 *Capital Gains Tax and the Small Business*
Leaflet IR24 *Class 4 National Insurance Contributions*
Leaflet IR28 *Starting in Business*
Leaflet IR37 *Income Tax and Capital Gains Tax Appeals*
Leaflet IR53 *Thinking of Taking Someone On?*
Leaflet IR56 *Tax – Employed or Self-employed*
Leaflet IR56/NI39 *Tax: Employed or Self-employed?*
Leaflet IR57 *Thinking of Working for Yourself?*
Leaflet IR104 *Simple Tax Accounts*
Leaflet IR105 *How Your Profits are Taxed*
Leaflet P7 *Employers Guide to PAYE*
Leaflet IR106 *Capital Allowances for Vehicles and Machinery*

Customs and Excise VAT Offices
General Guide
The Ins and Outs of VAT
Keeping Records and Accounts
Printed and Similar Matter
Scope and Coverage
Self-supply (Stationery)
Should I Be Registered for VAT?

Department of Employment
These titles are part of a series:

Employees Rights on Insolvency of Employer
Employment Rights for the Expectant Mother
Employment Rights on the Transfer of an Undertaking: The Law on Unfair Dismissal – Guidance for Small Firms
Itemised Pay Statement
Written Statement of Main Terms and Conditions of Employment

Health and Safety Commission
Advice to Employers
Advice to the Self-employed
The 1974 Act Outlined

Magazines of general use and interest

Computer Shopper (PO Box 320, London N21 2NB) A monthly run-down of the latest computers, printers, software etc: choc full of competitive advertisements.

For reviews of current PCs/software try:

What Personal Computer? (EMAP Publications)
PC User (EMAP Publications)
Personal Computer World (EMAP Publications)
Which Computer? (EMAP Publications)
Which Word Processor? (EMAP Publications)

For more advanced computers and applications:

Micro Decision (VNU Business Publications, 32-34 Broadwick Street, London W1A 2HG) Available only by complimentary subscription to small/medium-sized business managers.

Appendix
Guide to Layout and Sample Formats

Dissertations, theses and manuscripts

Universities, polytechnics and colleges normally provide their degree students with a detailed specification for the format of dissertations and theses. This normally comprises instructions for page numbering, margins, footnotes, spacing, layout of bibliography, quotations and so on. Publishers almost always provide similar instructions for their authors. Hence, if you are asked to produce a dissertation, thesis, manuscript or play script, you should ask if your customer has received specific format instructions. Once you have produced one or two dissertations for a particular university, you will know its requirements. It is a good idea to keep a note of these as many students mislay, or fail to receive, their dissertation typing instructions.

Dissertations and theses
As a general guide, print on one side of A4 paper and leave a margin of about 35 mm on the left and about 25 mm on the other three sides. Dissertations and theses are normally bound (often with a simple grip binding) on the left and the extra margin width allows for this. Double-space the main text throughout and leave an extra line (or two) between paragraphs and between headings/subheadings and text. Headings, subheadings etc should be standardised throughout the text. Quotations, footnotes, references and bibliographies are normally single-spaced. Indent quotations about five spaces (at both sides) as well as any footnotes and references which appear in the main body of the text.

References to other works (eg book titles), species names and some medical terms are conventionally underlined (the student should already have done this on the handwritten copy).

Numbering normally starts on the first page of the first chapter (this is usually preceded by a facing page showing the title, author, date, university and so on; an acknowledgements page and a contents page). You will have to prepare the contents page last as you will need to insert the relevant page numbers and you won't know these until the end. Start each new chapter on a new page.

Normally, two copies are required for submission and the student may wish to retain a third copy.

Book manuscripts

Book manuscripts are conventionally double-spaced throughout (including quotations, references and bibliography) on one side of A4 paper with four spaces between paragraphs, headings and text, and subheadings and text. This additional space makes it easier for the editor and typesetter to read and mark comments on the script as well as allowing plenty of space for clear alterations or corrections. Likewise, leave generous margins all round and especially on the left where there should be extra space to allow for the typesetter's clip to hold the manuscript without obscuring the text. Publishers usually prefer manuscripts to be printed using a typeface with regular rather than 'proportional' character spacing (ie each character taking up the same amount of space) as this makes it easier for the typesetter to estimate the amount of text on a page.

All pages should be numbered, preferably consecutively. Occasionally, the title page, preface, lists of contents etc are numbered separately in roman numerals. Page numbers should be in the top right-hand corner. It is normally acceptable to insert extra pages later on so long as these are numbered appropriately (340a, 340b and so on in between pages 340 and 341 with a note on pages 340 *and* 341 that 340a and 340b follow and precede respectively).

Two copies are normally required by the publisher (and the author would be well advised to keep a copy for himself).

Ask the author for a copy of the publisher's house rules regarding abbreviation, spelling, hyphenation, composite words, numbering, dates, addresses, titles and the use of capital letters. If the author has not followed the publisher's house rules, you can offer to make the appropriate corrections (but be sure to charge extra) but remember to be consistent – it's not good enough to type 'book-keeping' on one page and 'bookkeeping' on the next.

Play scripts

You may be asked to prepare these for local amateur dramatic societies or, more rarely, for professional playwrights (who will have more stringent rules for the layout of the script). In general, you should leave a very generous margin on the left (40 mm or more): this allows sufficient room for binding and leaves the text clear for the performers to read. Separate dialogue from the rest of the script (scene changes, character descriptions, details of action, motivation, behaviour and so on) by leaving a space and indenting from the left as shown below:

> TYPIST   Leave a space between dialogue and
>
> the rest of the script. Type
>
> character names in capitals. Number
>
> scene changes sequentially. Double-
>
> space the dialogue for ease of
>
> reading.

You should also consider the time it will take you to type a play script when you estimate your charges. It is much more difficult to type colloquial speech, for example, than it is to type literary, academic or business speech.

The number of copies required will be determined by whether the play is for the direct use of an amateur dramatic society or is the preliminary script for a professional play, film or television programme.

Business letters

For business people who do not have fixed ideas about the layout of their correspondence, you could provide a variety of sample displays.

Style

The principal popular letter styles are fully blocked and semi-blocked (see figures on pages 182 and 183). A fully blocked letter is quicker and easier to key and also allows you to position the address so that a window envelope can be used (which provides a further saving in time since you don't have to print the address on an envelope).

Letters should be laid out and spaced according to their length.

Punctuation
Many businesses now use open punctuation. This means that no

SUPERSONIC VAN HIRE LIMITED
Any Street, Anytown

Fully blocked letter

SUPERSONIC VAN HIRE LIMITED
Any Street, Anytown

Semi-blocked letter

punctuation is inserted in the date, names, addresses, salutation and complimentary close, or after contractions. This has the advantage of saving time but some people do not like it. Be guided by the preference of your customer.

Paragraphing
A new paragraph is used whenever the subject changes. Many business people are hopeless at paragraphing and will appreciate your help with this. Avoid a letter in the form of a single long paragraph. Almost all letters can be broken down into at least three parts: the opening remarks, the bulk of the information being conveyed and a summation requesting action.

The subscription
When the letter starts with 'Dear Sir/Madam' the subscription is 'Yours faithfully'; when the salutation is 'Dear Mr Jones' the subscription is 'Yours sincerely'.

Agendas and minutes

You may be asked to prepare agendas and minutes of meetings for local clubs and organisations. Usually, the customer will provide an old agenda or set of minutes for your guidance: if so, follow the layout of the previous ones. Be certain to ask how many copies will be required (normally each member of the committee has one and one should be retained by the chairman for filing). These are the standard headings that commonly appear on the agenda:

1. The place, date and time of the meeting
2. Apologies for absence
3. Minutes of last meeting (these will be read, confirmed as correct and signed by the chairman)
4. Business arising from the minutes
5. Main business of the meeting (possibly several sections on this)
6. Any other matters
7. Date of next meeting

The minutes of a meeting record the name of the board or committee, the place, date and time of the meeting. The members present are listed followed by those who send apologies for absence. (Take care to ensure that you can read the names of committee members: if necessary, ask your customer to print these separately.) The minutes then follow the items on the agenda noting, in particular, any decisions that have been made. Occasionally, an 'Action' column separated from the minutes by at least three spaces is used.

Curriculum vitae

The layout of CVs can vary but the essential ingredients generally remain the same. Most comprise the following general sections:

- Personal details
- Educational qualifications
- Professional qualifications and memberships
- Employment history
- Interests and hobbies
- Referees

You will want to tailor each CV to suit individual customers and their employment aspirations. However you lay out the CV, you should aim to stress the applicant's strongest features and, if the applicant is applying for a particular type of job, emphasise qualities, qualifications and experience relevant to that particular career. Many people have difficulty in presenting information of this nature in the most attractive and readable form. So if you have good compositional English skills, you should be able to make a great success of a CV production service.

Your charge will depend on whether you are simply typing up the customer's own handwritten résumé or whether you are actually composing the CV from the customer's details.

Make up a book of samples showing a variety of layouts (block out actual names/addresses to preserve confidentiality) and offer a selection of paper weights and colours. Include extra sheets for handwritten covering letters and matching envelopes for an 'executive' service.

Two examples are offered on pages 186 and 187. Try to avoid having your customer's CV extending beyond three or four pages. At this length, your customer risks boring a potential employer with detail, unless the job is very specialised and a long breakdown of work experience is called for.

Basic curriculum vitae

Name:	JOHN DOE	Date of Birth	15.05.1956
Address:	46 Any Street Anytown ANY 156	Age: Status:	35 Single
Telephone:	(0101) 34567	Health:	Excellent
		Nationality:	British

Schools/College Attended	Qualification Received
Anytown Grammar School Anytown 1967-1972	GCE 'O' levels in: Mathematics (A), English (B), Geography (B) and Physics (C)
Anytown College of FE Anytown 1972-1974	HNC Accounting

Employer/Dates	Position/Responsibility
AB Jones History Anytown 1980-present	OFFICE MANAGER Supervising staff of six. Total administrative control of advertising, sales, purchases, payroll and bookkeeping.
Anytown Council Council Anytown 1974-1980	CLERICAL ASSISTANT (1974-1976). Making up wage packets for 230 employees. Keeping employee records. CLERICAL OFFICER (1976-1980). Keeping inventory records, preparing and checking purchase orders, processing payments and receipts.

Interests and Hobbies

Squash, swimming, travel, reading and home-computing.

Referees

Available as required.

Expanded curriculum vitae

This would have the same personal and educational details as the 'basic' CV but would include an expanded section detailing work or other relevant experience as well as emphasising any particular aptitudes and abilities as shown below.

Employment History and Experience

1980   AB Jones Hosiery
                                  Anytown

As OFFICE MANAGER, my responsibilities include supervising six clerical staff and all personnel work (interviewing, hiring, disciplining and dismissing staff) for a total staff of 43. I also have total administrative control over advertising (current annual budget £5000 pa), sales, purchases, payroll and bookkeeping. The company's turnover is approximately £350,000. Notice required – 1 month.

1974–1980   Anytown Council Council
                                  Anytown

I began work with the Anytown Council Council as CLERICAL ASSISTANT in the wages section. My duties included calculating wages/NI/PAYE/superannuation/additions and deductions for 230 employees as well as making up and distributing wage packets. In 1976, I was promoted to CLERICAL OFFICER in the finance section. My responsibilities included maintaining inventory records, organising and supervising the annual stock-take, preparing and checking purchase orders, and processing payments and receipts.

Supplementary Information

I hold a full, clean, current driving licence and speak fluent French and some Spanish. I am currently attending a part-time 12-week course (evenings) in Modern Office Automation and Computerisation at the Anytown College of Further Education.

I am self-motivated, communicate well with people at all levels and feel that I have the drive, ability, qualifications and experience necessary to make a valuable contribution towards the development of your company.

Index

accessories 96-7, 144-5
accountant *see* advice
accounts, annual 54-8
advertising:
   classified 71
   direct mail 73-4
   effective 72
   free 69
   shop window 70-71
   word of mouth 74
advice:
   accountants 155
   bank managers 155-6
   insurance brokers 157
   solicitors 157
   sources of 46-7, 158
agendas and minutes, layout of 184-5
alterations *see* corrections and alterations
ASCII codes 95
audio-typing:
   dictating machines 105-7
   offering service 141-2

bank account 50-51, 129-31
bank manager *see* advice
bookkeeping:
   offering service 137-8
   records 44-5, 51-4
business, buying existing 158-9
business cards 75-6
business name 43-4
business structure:
   limited company 38-9
   partnership 37-8, 152-4
   sole trader 37-8

capital allowances 57
   computation 61
capital gains tax 41-2
cash:
   paying by 129
   raising 48-9
charging:
   calculating prices 33-4, 67-8
   for alterations 125-6
   methods of 65-7
   special offers 76
   undercharging 68
collection and delivery, offering service 135-6
commitment:
   personal 13-14
   time 12, 33-4
community charge 40-41
competitors, keeping abreast of 28-9, 68
computers:
   choice of 86-8
   disks 88-9
   offering services 139-40
   purchasing 86-8
   testing 90
contract of employment *see* staff
corrections and alterations: 117-18
   charging for 125-6
   common errors 127
   whose fault? 126
costs:
   as business expands 163
   running 65-7
   start-up 26-7
credit cards 130-31

creditors, paying 132
customers:
  being paid by 129-32
  dealing with 18, 115-16, 119-23
  providing good image to 77-8
  range of 12-13, 29-31
CV (curriculum vitae):
  offering service 31
  layout of 185-7

depreciation:
  estimating 57
  in tax computation 61
desk-top publishing 142-5
dictating machines 105-7
  see also audio-typing
direct mail see advertising
dissertations and theses:
  attracting custom 12-13, 30, 70
  competitors' services 29
  layout of 179-80
drawings 58
DSS, informing of commencement 40

electronic mail 140
employees see staff
Enterprise Allowance Scheme 80
equipment:
  checklist 113
  essential start-up 25-6
  furniture and fittings 80-83, 162
  hiring or leasing 110-11
  maintenance agreements 89, 91, 159
  setting up office 79-80, 161-3
  small items of 108-10
  see also computers, dictating machines, facsimile, photocopiers, printers, telephone answering machines
errors see corrections and alterations

estimating 65-7, 116-17
  see also charges, costs

facsimile, offering service 140
finance, business plan 34-7
forecasting, financial 37

grants, local authority 49

handwriting, bad 122-3
health and safety see staff
hints:
  general tips 133-4
  time saving 115-19
hire purchase and leasing 49, 110-11

income tax 58-9
  changes to rates 64
  computation 61, 62
  paying 62
Inland Revenue, informing of commencement 40
  see also income tax
insurance: 45-6
  brokers 157-8
  car 45

law:
  employment 166-9
  partnership 37-8
  self-employment 37, 40, 43
leasing see hire purchase and leasing
letters, style of 181-4
limited company see business structure
loans 48-9

manuscripts, layout of 180
market research, assessing demand 28-31
marketing 76-7
  see also advertising, market research
minutes see agendas and minutes, layout of

… Index 191

mistakes *see* corrections and alterations
mobile secretarial service 136-7
  see also collection and delivery; insurance, car
mouse *see* accessories

National Insurance:
  changes in rates 64
  classes of 59
  computation 62
  exemption from 60-61
  paying 59, 62
  self-employed 59-60

office equipment *see* equipment
overdraft 48-9

partnership *see* business structure
PAYE 54
  see also staff
pensions 64-5
photocopiers 101-5
  offering service 102, 135
planning permission 41
playscripts, layout of 180-81
postal services:
  operation of 31
  paying for 131
premises 159-62
pricing *see* charging
printers 91-5
profit:
  calculating 58
  tax on drawings 58
proof-reading:
  offering service 146-7
  why essential 126-7

rates, business 41
recruitment *see* staff
retaining fee 41

scanners *see* accessories
skills:
  acquiring new 21, 24
  essential 21-4
  personal 17-21
  typing/wordprocessing 22-3
sole trader *see* business structure
solicitors *see* advice
specialising in one service:
  advertising 32-3
  dangers of 32
  need for flexibility 127-9
  skills, need for 32-3
spelling, grammar, punctuation 23
staff:
  contract of employment 166-7
  discipline and dismissal 168-9
  discrimination 166
  Employment Training Scheme 164
  health and safety 169
  hours of work 167-8
  legislation for 169
  PAYE 54, 167
  records for 54
  selecting 164-5
stock *see* accessories, equipment, supplies
subcontracting 148-52
success, chances of 14
supplies, renewable 111-12, 162-3

tax *see* capital gains, income, Inland Revenue
teaching, keyboard skills 146
telephone:
  answering machines 107-8
  answering service 138
  conversion costs 80
  cordless 80
  dealing with calls 116
  extension 80
telex and teletex 140
Thomson local directory 69, 73
time, organising 114-18
  see also commitment, estimating
trading name *see* business name

translating 146
typewriters 83-4

Value Added Tax (VAT):
  advice 63-4
  change to rates 64
  keeping records 53
  registration 62-3

wages *see* staff
word-processing:
  who can run service? 11
  who needs service? 12
word processors:
  basic components of 85
  capabilities of 84-6
  programmes 12, 87, 97-101
  ready-made packages 87
  see also printers, computers
working from home:
  advantages 24
  capital gains tax 41-2
  community charge and rates 40-41
  disadvantages 24-5
  neighbours 42-3
  planning permission 41
work form 123-5

Yellow Pages 69-70, 73